COLERIDGE
ON IMAGINATION

COLERIDGE
ON
IMAGINATION

BY

I. A. RICHARDS, Litt.D.

LONDON
ROUTLEDGE & KEGAN PAUL LTD
BROADWAY HOUSE: 68–74 CARTER LANE, E.C.4

First published 1934
Second edition 1950
Reprinted 1955
Third edition (with a new Foreword) 1962
Reprinted 1968

Printed by offset in Great Britain
by Alden & Mowbray Ltd
at the Alden Press, Oxford

SNB 7100 2031 7

[*face p. vii*]

As to me, my face, unless when animated by immediate eloquence, expresses great sloth, and great, indeed, almost idiotic good-nature. 'Tis a mere carcass of a face; fat, flabby, and expressive chiefly of inexpression. *Yet I am told that my eyes, eyebrows, and forehead are physiognomically good;* *but of this the deponent knoweth not.* *As to my shape, 'tis a good shape enough if measured, but my gait is awkward, and the walk of the whole man indicates* indolence capable of energies.

S. T. C.

In person he was a tall, dark, handsome young man, with long, black, flowing hair; eyes not merely dark, but black, and keenly penetrating; a fine forehead, a deep-toned harmonious voice; a manner never to be forgotten, full of life, vivacity, and kindness; dignified in person and, added to all these, exhibiting the elements of his future greatness.

The Rev. Leapidge Smith: *Leisure Hours,* 1870.

It is a good picture—certainly like you—but it wants character. . . . *It is a very agreeable picture, and it gives one pleasure to look at;* *but it is* Mr. Coleridge and not Coleridge. *You are in the drawing-room, and not in the vales of Quantock, or on the top of Skiddaw.*

Tom Poole.

CONTENTS

Mercy for praise, to be forgiven for fame
He asked, and hoped through Christ.   Do thou the same.

PREFACE

A LECTURER, who trusts that his audience will continue with him to the end of the course, can move by stages to his recommendations. So these chapters, like the lectures they have grown from, climb an intellectual hill, the views offered becoming, I hope, wider and clearer too as we ascend.

I should first indicate my approach to Coleridge—for there are many. I do not mean by this merely that he was a poet, a philosopher, a preacher, and a political theorist, as well as a critic. Nor do I mean that we may approve or disapprove, that we may consider him a genius and a pathological specimen; a methodologist and a muddler; a God-intoxicated man and a drug addict; a semasiologist and a victim of verbalism. . . . He has been treated sufficiently often as a human contradiction and as a biographers' puzzle. He has been pitied and patronised, condemned and defended enough. The literature on his 'case' must by now be nearly as voluminous as his own writings. I do not propose to add to it.

He was a semasiologist—aware, as few have been, that to ask about the meanings of words is to ask about everything. And I am assuming that his contributions towards this obscure, neglected, yet most central incipient science of the future are as important as he took them to be; that we still need to improve our understanding of language; that his unique combination of gifts enabled him to make some essential steps towards immense improvements; and that to attempt to take his work another step onwards is the best way of paying back a debt. But first a process of disentanglement must be gone through, for the disorder and complication of Coleridge's thought truly deserve their fame. I have not tried to sort out the strands in any *historical* fashion. That would be a more difficult venture in interpretation, and at present premature. My aim has been merely to extract, so far as I can, from the vast confusing network of his speculations and observations, those hypotheses which seem most likely to be useful in other hands. And my hope is to further their development into a co-operative technique of enquiry that may become entitled to be named a science.

A large part of the subject-matter of these enquiries is the behaviour of words in poetry, and many people, by training, must resent any suggestion that this should be treated by a science. I may anticipate here to point out that one of Coleridge's clearest and most certain principles preserves the autonomy both of the poet and the critic. "Could a rule be given from *without*, poetry would cease to be poetry, and sink into a mechanical art." None the less, a further development of Coleridge's method would fundamentally change current conceptions of the relation of Poetry to Life, and with this the contemporary tone of criticism. I do not mean that it would become more solemn or more acrimonious. Instead it would be more experimental and less self-assertive.

Most evaluative criticism is not statement or even attempted statement. It is either suasion, which is politics, or it is social communion. As social communion (in a lecture, for example) it is a method of preparing the scene and conducting the occasion, of maintaining the civilizing convention that things are well, of inducing a reassured, easy and decorously receptive mood. It is a stream of gestures or ceremonies, a spirit-calming and mildly stimulating ritual. If nothing happens, if nothing is said or nothing done, it is not the ritual that we should blame.

Experienced critics know this, more or less; though they do not often proclaim it so frankly as Professor Garrod at p. 158 in his *Poetry and Life*:

> More than any other of the literary kinds, criticism approximates to a *social* art—and this may be why the poets are unsuccessful in it. It is one of the most natural things in the world to discuss a book or a poem—far more natural than to write one. It is one of the most obvious of social acts or behaviours, but, like any other social act it perishes in the defect of those qualities which make a man interesting.

It perishes as one kind of 'social act', certainly; but has criticism no purposes beyond these? Are poetry and life only related so? Are there not other kinds of social acts, the invention of the radio valve, for example? And can we not hear the bombers being tuned up daily? "Criticism," says Mr Garrod, "is, or ought to be, one of the most delightful departments of literature; and that is especially true of the criticism of poetry." Could there be a more soothing piece of manners? Mr Garrod finds Hazlitt to be the greatest of English critics and Coleridge to lack 'just those qualities which make a critic.'

There are delights and delights evidently. Those which Coleridge offers are most often glimpses of a new possible theoretic order—behind them hope for new power thence; behind that again a regress of visions, of the rectified mind and the freed heart. But he gives these best in quintessences. I take what I can and dilute it to more convenient and more controllable measure. In doing so, I interpret him, of course, and I am not certain whether, historically, my interpretations 'wrong' him greatly or not. But every theoretical contribution to any study must, sooner or later, be wronged if it is successful in aiding further development.

My indebtedness to other students of Coleridge is chiefly to those who have made more of his immense body of writings available: to Mr Shawcross' edition of *Biographia Literaria*, to Mr Thomas Middleton Raysor's *Coleridge's Shakespearean Criticism*, to Miss Alice D. Snyder's *Coleridge on Logic and Learning* and *S. T. Coleridge's Treatise on Method*, and to Mr Earl Leslie Griggs' *Unpublished Letters of Samuel Taylor Coleridge*; but most to Ernest Hartley Coleridge for *Anima Poetae* and *The Letters*. My thanks are due to Dr Walter Holcroft Cam for permission to reproduce 'the German portrait,' and to the Clarendon Press for the loan of the block. It represents Coleridge at the time when all his important ideas were first taking clear form.

CAMBRIDGE,   I. A. R.
October 1934

PREFACE TO THE SECOND EDITION

This re-issue has afforded a welcome opportunity to clarify my interpretation with the aid of materials made available since I wrote—notably Miss Kathleen Coburn's edition of Coleridge's Philosophical Lectures 1818–19.

What now seems clearer to me is Coleridge's accord, at his best, with *The Republic*. His doctrine of "the component faculties of the human mind and their comparative rank and importance" is Plato's —including the delicate relations of Will and Reason. He is answering Plato's challenge to the friends of Poetry through a refinement and re-application of Plato's own thought. The coadunating imagination is a close analogue, if no more, to the synoptic activity of "the true music of dialectic". I have written on this, however, in *How to Read a Page*, which contains further experiments with some of Coleridge's methods.

I. A. R.

CAMBRIDGE, MASSACHUSETTS,
October 1949

FOREWORD TO THIRD EDITION

This reprinting gave me a welcome opportunity. Watching the immense growth in Coleridge scholarship through the decades since the book was written, I have felt that a Foreword was needed to tell the reader what all this work has done for the Coleridge whose positions I was attempting to plot. In an inspired moment I wondered if the generosity of the best balanced and most informed of Coleridgeans could be stretched so far as to write this for me—with the happy outcome that follows.

On the weightiest point which Miss Coburn raises —my "Hartley to Kant" sentence—I find this to say. However it may have been written, it is best *read*, I think, not as history, but as intellectual topography. I knew just enough about history not to suppose I could write that. Miss Coburn has, I think, now guarded us against misconceiving Coleridge here— and that is what matters. My deep debt to her includes the reviviscence of a hope that in its new form this book may continue that *use* of Coleridge we have at heart.

I.A.R.

CAMBRIDGE, MASSACHUSETTS
January. 1960

Dear I. A. R.

You ask me to write you a kind of foreword telling you briefly about all the things I disagree with—or as you delicately put it—anything I feel "should be adjusted." Then, you say, you won't have to make so many changes inside. Now it would take an Irishwoman to understand what a Welshman could mean by the like of that. A foreword of a kind indeed! I thought a foreword was intended to ease the reader gently into the book, to tell what sort of book it is and what it isn't, what he can and must not expect. But you in fact want to say—or want me to say, what is even more calamity-seeking—this is the kind of book it is and this much of it is dubious, or at least, questionable, and do not say I did not warn you!

This third edition is being reproduced by offset, which, you say, rules out extensive changes or numerous small ones. But I have a notion, you being the dialectical sort of person you are, that you enjoy the excuse for a process of argument rather than a battle to the death and a *final* text. Coleridge, too, at his best, thrived on the dynamic of contraries and contradictions, never finding any one church, political party, social theory, or philosophical creed to satisfy his sense of the subtleties of the human condition; and so this stratagem of writing a perverse foreword chiefly to raise objections, and by the hindsight of twenty-five years, is too Coleridgean a game to be given up by default.

Besides I should like, for other reasons also, to have a stab at this sort of foreword. Aside from the great compliment of the thing to me, there is by implication a stimulating tribute to the state of scholarship in our time; and to the reader as well, in the assumption that he will understand and even like to witness our struggle to get at a bit of the truth

about Coleridge—imagination—language—the attempts of the human race to save itself by adequate
articulation—however we define or expand the problem you have set before us.

You ask me to sum up my disagreements. Perhaps
you are like the fly that lights on the fly-swatter with
which one is trying to demolish him. But no one who
knows you would ever allow me any truth in this,
nor am I so foolish as to dream of attacking a moun-
taineer like you with a fly-swatter.

No, a better metaphor for the case is that you, an
experienced climber who took me up a Coleridge
mountain some twenty-five years ago, are now asking
me what I see from there after a quarter of a century
of scrambling on various ranges of hills on my own,
and especially to point out, if I can, anything that was
misted over then and is more visible now. This alarming challenge I respond to—not because of the thick-
ness of the disagreements with you, but because of the
far-reaching importance of *Coleridge on Imagination*.

Two books changed the face of Coleridge studies
in the 1930's: Lowes's *Road to Xanadu*, and yours.
Lowes taught us a lot about Coleridge and especially
he made plain and specific beyond all shadow of
doubting, the immense variety of the materials of
poetry; in a measure he painted Coleridge's chaos,
its conscious aspects. Your *Coleridge on Imagination*
gave us a new look at Coleridge, and also at the
imagination, each as it were, in the mathematical
use of the word, the function of the other. The fer-
tility of your view—this *use* of Coleridge—is without
end. Anyhow, this was for me the great excitement
of your book—the expression of a great optimistic
organic dynamic view of poetry, of Coleridge, and
even of the human potential itself, in its broadest
terms. So I have only gratitude for your book in its

fundamentals.

Now to the quarrelling.

It is almost entirely a matter of details, but perhaps, and the more I think about it the farther it reaches, the one larger issue is suggested by the phrase "Coleridge's conversion from Hartley to Kant" (p. 17). By implication this appears as early as page 11, where his "renunciation of Hartley as a guide in psychology" is linked with Coleridge's return from Germany; and on page 59 (in that particularly interesting third chapter) the alleged transition takes this form: "The passage from the conception of the mind's doings as Fancy to that of the creative Imagination is the passage from Hartley to Kant." My objection is hydra-headed. Hartley and Kant are in no sense termini, as of course need not be said, and even if they were there are others in between, especially Berkeley; also Spinoza, Plotinus, certain Schoolmen, Erasmus Darwin, and others with more or less oblique relations to it all—Gurke, Humphry Davy (very interested in poetry and imagination), Tom Wedgwood and his studies in perception, Cudworth, and the Cambridge Platonists. Some of the opposition, even Hobbes and Locke, left scars. But chiefly my point is that too much has been made of Hartley and far too much of Kant (one could wish perhaps in Coleridge's vision of things for more of Kant?) in the attempts to track down Coleridge's system. Coleridge began to suspect the soundness of his enthusiasm for Hartley as soon as he saw that Associationism in this form meant the passivity of the mind, a concept he rejected out of his own immediate experience. For allied reasons he objected to Erasmus Darwin's views, and read Baxter, and Cudworth, and Jeremy Taylor. We do not know exactly when he began to read Kant—on the margins of *Grundlegung zur Metaphysik der Sitten* in 1803, he makes the charge that "in Psychology Kant is but suspicious Authority." Later he became more emphatic still on this point.

I am inclined to hold to my view expressed a few years ago, that Coleridge, at some time between the 1809–10 *Friend* and the writing of *Biographia Literaria* in 1815, took up Schelling as offering more scope for emotion in the aesthetic scheme of things than Kant, but before he had finished dictating the *Biographia Literaria* to John Morgan he knew (depressed and in defeat as he was at that time) that there was little reality in that form of transcendentalism for him, and he went back to Kant. And to Plato. By the 1818 *Friend* and the "Essay on Method" he is his own man again. So far as he was guided by systems, would you not agree that Coleridge was first and last a Platonist—with the checks and counter-checks against Plato's "dear gorgeous nonsense" offered by Kant, and still more by an observing eye, by a preternaturally acute proneness to self-analysis, and by something essentially pragmatic in the air—Wordsworth, Poole, Davy, even Lamb, and the English traditional empirical practicality itself?

You are too generous to Professor Wellek's youthful thesis, *Kant in England* (your footnotes on pages 10 and 180), for Wellek is there not "fair to Coleridge" in his interpretation either of his words or of his unsystematic position. He appears to blame Coleridge for (a) taking too much from Kant, (b) not taking enough. But the Procrustean beds of European systems cannot be pulled out from under S.T.C., for he never lay on them. Nor is this a question of English versus German philosophy. Coleridge was not a systematic philosopher, though frequently he longed to build a system on a mammoth scale—to take in everything—science and poetry and politics and morals too. As you so deftly point out. And it is in the interests of this total, complicated, subtle, unsystematic, illuminating vision of him, as a functional human being and thinker, that I distrust this Hartley-to-Kant description. We need to emend this old formula if not abandon it altogether, and you as much as anyone have made this necessary. So my point I think is cogent in your whole case.

For the rest, nothing but small points. On page 20 pursuing your "genial criticism" in Coleridge's sense, could you not qualify your statement—very true but not the whole truth—to the effect that "in much that Coleridge wrote later (especially in the *Biographia Literaria* [written 1815, published 1817]) he . . . seems merely to be re-formulating old problems"? I should like to put in a word here for the "Essay on Method" in *Encyclopaedia Metropolitana* edition, or the third volume of *The Friend*. For one thing this is one of the freshest signs of that resurgence of creative power that came with his finding a haven at Highgate; and it provides also the clearest way out of the metaphysical muddle of the undigested Schelling passages in the *Biographia*, in fact celebrates his abandonment of Schelling altogether. The "Essay on Method" I find a most useful and significant document.

In your magnificent third chapter, Coleridge's own distinction between discovery and invention would be a clarifying addition (p. 49)—if I may brashly refer to *Coleridge Notebooks*, entries 387, 930, and 950 and their notes? On page 55 I feel Fichte should come in, as he did at least briefly but effectively for Coleridge in his view of the Self as Act, and knowing as Act, and on page 66 I am sure you do not mean to suggest (compare p. 68) that as early as 1801 Coleridge's *formulations* were Schellingian (see p. 65), but your words *could* convey this.

About metre in Chapter V, I will go along with you entirely so long as you do not imply, say on page 119, that Coleridge was not occupied with the hard technical footwork of metrics. The *Notebooks* alone would give you the lie at this point: see e.g. entry 2224 in the forthcoming volume and even the metrical entries in Volume I.

On page 214 you quote a famous passage; the full reading in *Coleridge Notebooks*, I, 383, significantly does not upset your applecart, as it has so many others. I do not understand fully your objection in Chapter VI (p. 28) to "identifying Good Sense . . . with 'the principles of grammar, logic and psychology' " [not as you and Coleridge, but as *most*, alas, will understand them—I.A.R.]. Does not Coleridge mean the same as you when you say (on p. 140): "the judgment that a passage is good is an act of living. The examination and description of its merits is an act of theory"? I am not objecting here, just puzzled. I take Coleridge to mean, that when we say this is a good poem, when a poem appeals to our good sense of what we want of poetry, we shall find on further theoretical probing, that the poem in question obeys no "mechanical rule from without" but the laws of its medium (language), the laws of communication (logic), and the laws of life applicable to the poet and his audience alike, i.e. the laws that govern every experiencing human being, the laws of psychology. Am I failing to understand your point? [No, most helpfully clarifying it!—I.A.R.]

None of my questions touches your basic conception, that Coleridge's thoughts about language, poetry, life itself, are deeply rooted in psychological awareness, dynamic in character, inseparable in themselves from the other parts of the whole story. One of your remarks I must treasure is the daring sentence

(p. 67), "Were Coleridge alive now, he would, I hope, be applauding and improving doctrines of the type he, as a metaphysician, thought least promising in his own day." This is I believe a profound truth, and a statement Coleridge himself would understand. (In fact, I am not sure you didn't learn it from him!)

You have yourself raised questions about the Benthamitish part of your book. I do not wish them away —for this very reason—nor the last chapter either which you threaten to slough off. There are valuable facets of truth in them about aspects of Coleridge's thinking that have not been looked at often enough. It is true that he was an incorrigible Platonist with his eye fixed on some great, ineffable, undefinable, unknowable Idea of Man, God, the Good, the True, the Beautiful, all in the capital letters of some more Absolute Everest of Being. Is it not also true, that he was the inquiring spirit Mill describes, asking "what is the meaning of it?" As he searched out his toe-holds he was, certainly, full of the joy of your "journeys without destinations," in his own words, "the pleasurable activity of mind excited by the attractions of the journey itself."

KATHLEEN COBURN

COLERIDGE ON IMAGINATION

CHAPTER I

THE FIRST RANGE OF HILLS

Though I might find numerous precedents, I shall not desire the reader to strip his mind of all prejudices, or to keep all prior systems out of view during his examination of the present. For in truth, such requests appear to me not much unlike the advice given to hypochondriacal patients in Dr Buchan's domestic medicine ; *videlicit*, to preserve themselves uniformly tranquil and in good spirits.—*Biographia Literaria*.

"At the same time that we were studying the Greek Tragic Poets, he (Bowyer, Head Master of the Grammar School, Christ's Hospital) made us read Shakespeare and Milton as lessons: and they were the lessons, too, which required most time and trouble to *bring up* so as to escape his censure. I learnt from him, that Poetry, even that of the loftiest and, seemingly, that of the wildest odes, had a logic of its own, as severe as that of science; and more difficult, because more subtle, more complex, and dependent upon more, and more fugitive, causes." Coleridge's studies in this severe logic, his inquiry into these multiple and fugitive causes occupied the best years of his life. The methods he employed and the results that he reached are the subject of this Essay. To neither, in spite of the large literature that has accumulated about him, has justice been done.

A   1

He was naturally a psychologist, abnormally aware of and curious about the happenings in his own mind, with a delight in and a talent for systematic thinking that are as uncommon. He had, moreover, a mind which gave him, in its incessant activity, more remarkable material to inquire into than is ordinarily combined with such a capacity to inquire. He lived at a time when a deep and general change was occurring in man's conceptions of himself and of his world, and he spent his powers upon the elaboration of a speculative apparatus that would be a kind of microscope with which to study this change and others. It is not an easy instrument to use. It needs adjustment and perhaps some re-designing. I am not, in what follows, very much concerned to present Coleridge's theory in the exact form in which he built it. We can show, I think, more respect for his achievement and for the importance of the purposes to which he gave so much of his life by using his drafts and sketches to construct a derived instrument. But the principle will be his, and where terms, distinctions and other technical devices are being used that have developed since Coleridge, the departures will be easily pointed out.

He had been a preternaturally reflective schoolboy, in his early teens "delving into the unwholesome quicksilver mines of metaphysic depths." From "this preposterous pursuit" he was rescued, he tells us twenty-nine years later, "partly indeed by an accidental introduction to an amiable family, chiefly

however by the genial influence" of Bowles' sonnets.
Defending these at Cambridge and later, he constantly appealed to "TRUTH, NATURE, LOGIC and
the LAWS OF UNIVERSAL GRAMMAR", still very much
in Capital Letters. "Actuated, too, by my former
passion for metaphysical investigations; I laboured
at a solid foundation, on which permanently to
ground my opinions, in the component faculties of
the human mind itself, and their comparative
dignity and importance. According to the faculty
or source, from which the pleasure given by any
poem or passage was derived, I estimated the merit
of such poem or passage."

Labour upon this foundation went on for a while
under the guidance of Hartley:

> he of mortal kind
> Wisest, he first who marked the ideal tribes
> Up the fine fibres through the sentient brain.

I shall try later (Chapter III) to show why
Coleridge at the crisis of his speculative life turned
away from Hartley, from whom he had learnt so
much—whose doctrines, whether we derive them
from Hartley or not, must be borne in mind if we
are to reconstruct Coleridge's thought.

But I must delay first for a few pages to complain
of the very common and rather lazy assumption
that intellectual labour will not help the critic.
I will quote from Mr Eliot an example of what has
become a general custom among literary men in
discussing Coleridge. "Nor am I sure," he says,
"that Coleridge learned so much from German

philosophers, or earlier from Hartley, as he thought he did; what is best in his criticism seems to come from his own delicacy and subtlety of insight as he reflected upon his own experience of writing poetry" (*The Use of Poetry*, p. 80). Yes. But is it an accident that this very peculiar kind of insight is found in Coleridge? His philosophic pre-occupations cannot be separated from it. The speculations and the insight incessantly prompt one another. The insight was the stimulus to the speculation and the speculation the instrument of the insight. "By *meditation*, rather than by *observation?* And by the latter in consequence of the former? As eyes, for which the former has pre-determined their field of vision, and to which, as to its organ, it communicates a microscopic power" (*B. L.*, II, 64. Shawcross' Edition). No one who is aware of Coleridge's problems or of the delicacy and subtlety with which he explored them will suppose that he could avoid these dealings with philosophy. He might, perhaps, have halted in his system-building sooner than he did (say about 1808). Yet can we blame him for continuing? What he had already extracted from 'vain Philosophy's aye-babbling spring' was enough to make anyone go on in hope of more.

It is easy for us *now*—when some fragments of his results in corrupted forms have passed into the general current of thought—to pretend that the toil which produced them was superfluous. But we shall not realize what we might gain from Coleridge without some equivalent trouble. We can neither recapture what his insight gave him nor develop it further, unless, in new terms perhaps, we make a similar effort of thought. The chief weakness of our best criticism today is the pretence that fundamental matters can be profitably discussed without prolonged and technical thinking.

What has been done by people who have found themselves discussing Coleridge has been, usually I think, to put a ring-fence round a very small part of his thought, and say, "We will keep inside this and leave the transcendental and the analytic discussions to someone else." But this practice results in what is essentially a fraud. The thought so fenced off ceases to be Coleridge's and becomes something much less interesting. It will therefore be well for me to state that I propose here to take all the parts of Coleridge's thinking that seem to me relevant to his criticism, and to treat them as an exercise ground for interpretation. I assume that Coleridge's great merit as a critic—a merit unique among English critics—is the strenuous persistence with which he reflected philosophically upon criticism. Is there not something a little ridiculous in saying, "What a fine critic! What a pity he thought so hard about Poetry!"?

He had, it is true, extraordinary gifts as a poet and a reader. But these gifts would not have produced what he has given us if he had not gone on, from his fourteenth year, thinking about poetry with an assiduity and enterprise that cannot be matched in the biography of another critic. The result is that his remarks have often a definite charge of elaborate meaning which we will pass by if we read him as we might quite properly read others. For example: In Chapter XV of the *Biographia* he comments upon the "perfect sweetness of the versification in the 'Venus and Adonis' as a characteristic of original poetic genius." "The sense of musical delight," he remarks, "with the power of producing it is a gift of the imagination." If someone else had said that, we might be quite justified in passing it by as *just the right sort of thing to be said.* We might have agreed that it seemed generally true and gone on our way satisfied that none of our notions need be disturbed.

But, since it is Coleridge who is speaking, we shall find, if we look into it and really ask what he is saying, that it is as far from being a commonplace as anything could be. We shall find that it is an application of two startling and fundamental theories —one (under the heading of 'imagination') about nothing less than the nature of consciousness itself; the other ('the power of producing it') about the conditions of communication between minds.[1]

I shall be coming back to linger with these theories—so let us not delay with them here.

It will be well, however, to say something more against the view that Coleridge's philosophy can in some way be separated from his thinking. Those who have supposed so have been numerous, and

[1] Cf. *B. L.*, I, 168.

they persist. Some even will quote Coleridge himself in their support. "It is time to tell the truth," he wrote, "though it requires some courage to avow it in an age and country, in which disquisitions on all subjects, not privileged to adopt technical terms or scientific symbols, must be addressed to the PUBLIC. I say then, that it is neither possible or necessary for all men, or for many, to be PHILOSOPHERS" (*B. L.*, I, 164). No more, under present social and economic conditions, is it possible for all men, or for many, to know anything about poetry. But this does not show either that such a state of affairs is tolerable to those who are aware that it can be changed, or that knowledge about poetry can be gained without "a *philosophic* (and inasmuch as it is actualized by an effort of freedom, an *artificial*) *consciousness*, which lies beneath or (as it were) *behind* the spontaneous consciousness natural to all reflective beings."

This passage comes just before the celebrated allegory:

The first range of hills, that encircles the scanty vale of human life, is the horizon for the majority of its inhabitants. On *its* ridges the common sun is born and departs. From *them* the stars rise, and touching *them* they vanish. By the many, even this range, the natural limit and bulwark of the vale, is but imperfectly known. Its higher ascents are too often hidden by mists and clouds from uncultivated swamps, which few have courage or curiosity to penetrate. To the multitude below these vapors appear, now as the dark haunts of terrific agents, on which none may intrude

7

with impunity; and now all *a-glow*, with colors not their own, they are gazed at as the splendid palaces of happiness and power. But in all ages there have been a few, who measuring and sounding the rivers of the vale at the feet of their farthest inaccessible falls have learned, that the sources must be far higher and far inward; a few, who even in the level streams have detected elements, which neither the vale itself or the surrounding mountains contained or could supply. How and whence to these thoughts, these strong probabilities, the ascertaining vision, the intuitive knowledge may finally supervene, can be learnt only by the fact.[1]

Many have enjoyed this passage; few have ventured seriously toward the test of the fact. Among these was Coleridge; on those ridges or in those mists and swamps, his waking life was spent; and it is our custom to scorn him for his 'selfish philosophizing', or to pity him for 'the dissipation and stupefaction of his powers'. If he had spent his time stamp-collecting or twiddling his thumbs instead, he would have escaped not a little abuse.

And here I have to dissent—with the least possible pugnacity—from some remarks of Sir Arthur Quiller-Couch in his Introduction to Mr Sampson's volume of *Selected Passages from Wordsworth and Coleridge.*

He tells us there to "cast back on our memories and to think that next to spring hats and parlour games, systems of philosophy are perhaps the most fugacious of all human toys? To those who listened

---

[1] *B. L.*, I, 164-166.

once and eagerly, how far and faint already sound
the echoes of Mansel, and Hegel plus Lewes plus
T. H. Green; counterchiming against Bentham,
John Stuart Mill, Herbert Spencer and Comte as
interpreted by the Positivists; Nietzsche, Bergson,
James have followed; and have passed, or are
passing; even Croce they tell me is in process of
being supplanted—'where are the snows of yester-
year?'" (p. xxxi).

'The most fugacious of all human toys'—'after
spring hats and parlour games'. Yes! if we take
them as 'lines of talk' to be acquired by those who
will be intellectually in the fashion—as such, the
amusement of these toys wanes fast and it is to be
wished that they were more fugacious. As haber-
dashery for the mental *arriviste*, gesture-suits for
up-to-date talkers, they are just as fugacious as
fashions in poetry. It takes no longer to learn to
manipulate a philosophy than to learn to admire
a kind of poetry. And there need be no more
insight into the philosophy than understanding of
the poetry. A little practice with the philosophy,
a little habituation to the poetry, are all that are
needed.

But we may regard philosophers in another way;
and then they will not seem so fugacious. No careful,
acute and resolute piece of thinking ever loses its
value—its power to be of use to mankind. (It is
the same with poetry; a good poem may lose its
public for generations—they being interested otherwise—but not its value for readers with the relevant

equipment.) It will perhaps have been noticed that Sir Arthur did not mention Plato and Aristotle among his fugacious philosophers. But every good philosopher stands with Plato and Aristotle; his work remains permanently as an aid in exploring the possibilities of our meanings. And often the very mistakes he made will be a large part of his value.

Coleridge was not, I suppose, a good philosopher;[1] he made too many mistakes *of the wrong kind*. He mixed with his philosophy too many things which did not belong to it, he let accidental and inessential prejudices too much interfere. In spite of them he took the psychology of the theory of poetry to a new level. For causes whose force will be experienced by anyone who follows Coleridge with any closeness he could not help adding into and developing again out of this relevant psychology a huge ill-assorted fabric of philosophic and theological beliefs which is not, I think, a relevant part of it. But it is, as I see it, an elaborated, transformed *symbol* of some parts of the psychology. And here is the modern reader's difficulty with Coleridge; that neither as theology (supposing him to admit such a subject

[1] See René Wellek, *Immanuel Kant in England*, chapter iii, "Samuel Taylor Coleridge and Kant," pp. 66-68, where the case against Coleridge as a philosopher is vigorously as well as fairly stated. But it is permissible to regard his ' little insight into the incompatibility of different kinds of thought ' as part of the secret of Coleridge's success in the theory of meanings. For a defence from an academic standpoint, see J. H. Muirhead, *Coleridge as Philosopher*, and " Metaphysician or Mystic," in *Coleridge Studies by Several Hands on the Hundredth Anniversary of his Death*, edited by Edmund Blunden and Earl Leslie Griggs.

as more than a study of symbolisms) nor as symbol, is this fabric satisfactory, or even intelligible, to him. Coleridge constantly presents it as though it were the matrix out of which he obtained his critical theories. But the critical theories can be obtained from the psychology without initial complication with the philosophical matter. They can be given all the powers that Coleridge found for them, without the use either literally, or symbolically, of the other doctrines. The psychology [1] and the metaphysics (and theology) are independent. For Coleridge's own thought, they were not; they probably could not be; to a later reader they may, and, as a rule, will be. The way to prevent the irrelevant matter from becoming at the outset an obstacle to an understanding of the psychology is to remember that special historical circumstances, temporary local conditions, shaped Coleridge's thought.

It seems to have taken its shape, as we are concerned with it, fairly suddenly with the renunciation of Hartley as a guide in psychology. This crisis occurred after his return from Germany during his first year at Greta Hall, Keswick, the first year of the century. His letters—to Godwin, to Poole, to Thelwall, to Sir Humphrey Davy—return again and

---

[1] Coleridge's footnote to 'psychological' (*Treatise on Method*, Snyder, 32): "We beg pardon for the use of this *insolens verbum*; but it is one of which our language stands in great need. We have no single term to express the Philosophy of the Human Mind: and what is worse, the Principles of that Philosophy are commonly called *Metaphysical*, a word of very different meaning."

again to the excitement of the questions that are haunting him:

To Godwin, September 1800.

I wish you to write a book on the power of the words, and the processes by which the human feelings form affinities with them. In short, I wish you to philosophize Horne Tooke's system, and to solve the great questions, whether there be reason to hold that an action bearing all the semblance of predesigning consciousness may yet be simply organic, and whether a series of such actions are possible? And close on the heels of this question would follow, Is Logic the *Essence* of thinking? In other words Is *Thinking* impossible without arbitrary signs? And how far is the word ' arbitrary ' a misnomer? Are not words, etc., parts and germinations of the plant? And what is the law of their growth? In something of this sort I would endeavour to destroy the old antithesis of Words and Things: elevating, as it were Words into Things and living things too. All the nonsense of vibrating, etc., you would of course dismiss. If what I have written appears nonsense to you, or common-place thoughts in a harlequinade of *outré* expressions, suspend your judgment till we see each other.

I can think of no passage in which so many of the fundamental problems of what is now known as semasiology are so brought together or so clearly stated. The last sentences prove that Coleridge had already turned away from Hartley, but the questions, especially the first, show the remarkable freedom with which the possibilities of his project were floating in Coleridge's mind.

To Davy, October 9, 1800.

The works which I gird myself up to attack as soon as money concerns will permit me are the *Life of Lessing*, and the *Essay on Poetry*. The latter is still more at my heart than the former: its title would be an essay on the elements of poetry,—it would be in reality a disguised system of morals and politics. When you write,—and do write soon,—tell me how I can get your essay on the nitrous oxide.

A rheumatic fever, followed by inflammation of the eyes gave him sleepless nights of extraordinary lucidity. He was struggling to finish *Christabel*:

To Davy, December 2, 1800.

For the last month I have been trembling on through the sands and swamps of evil and bodily grievance. My eyes have been inflamed to a degree that rendered reading and writing scarcely possible; and, strange as it seems, the act of metre composition, as I lay in bed, perceptibly affected them, and my voluntary ideas were every minute passing, more or less transformed into vivid spectra.

Between two requests for advice as to how 'a gentleman resident here, his name Calvert, an idle, good-hearted, and ingenious man' may best 'commence fellow-student with me and Wordsworth in chemistry'—which Coleridge considers 'knowledge so exceedingly important'—comes this:

To Davy, February 3, 1801.

For the next four or five months I fear, let me work as hard as I can, I shall not be able to do what my heart within me *burns* to do, that is, to *concentrate* my free mind to the affinities of the feelings with words and ideas under the title of 'Concerning Poetry, and the nature of the pleasures derived from it'. I have faith that I do understand the subject, and I am sure that if I write what I ought to do on it, this work would supersede all the books of metaphysics, and all the books of morals too. To whom shall a young man utter *his pride*, if not to a young man whom he loves. . . .

I have been *thinking* vigorously during my illness, so that I cannot say that my long, long wakeful nights have been all lost to me. The subject of my meditations has been the relations of thoughts to things; in the language of Hume, of ideas to impressions. I may be truly described in the words of Descartes: I have been 'res cogitans, id est, dubitans, affirmans, negans, pauca intelligens, multa ignorans, volens, nolens, imaginans etiam, et sentiens.' I please myself with believing that you will receive no small pleasure from the result of these broodings. . . . Every poor fellow has his proud hour sometimes, and this I suppose is mine.

One result of this ferment was a set of letters of prodigious length written during February to the Wedgwoods, his patrons, attacking Hobbes and Locke:

To Poole, February 13, 1801.

Since I have been at Keswick I have read a great deal, and my reading has furnished me with many reasons for being exceedingly suspicious of *supposed discoveries* in metaphysics.

A remark that it is wise to recall whenever the question is raised of S. T. C.'s indebtedness to others—not for formulations, he was an inveterate borrower there—but for insights. Part of his reading was Kant:

"Change of Ministry interests *me* not. I turn at times half reluctantly from Leibnitz or Kant even, to read a smoking new newspaper—such a *purus putus* metaphysician am I become."

By the middle of March the great change had happened and Coleridge was well launched:

To Poole, March 16, 1801.

The interval since my last letter has been filled up by me in the most intense study. If I do not greatly delude myself, I have not only *completely extricated the notions of time and space,* but have overthrown the doctrine of association, as taught by Hartley, and with it all the irreligious metaphysics of modern infidels—especially the doctrine of necessity. This I have *done*; but I trust that I am about to do more—namely, that I shall be able to evolve all the five senses, that is to deduce them from one sense, and to state their growth and the causes of their difference, and in this evolvement to solve the process of life and consciousness. *I write this to you only, and I pray you, mention what I have written to no one.* At Wordsworth's advice, or rather fervent entreaty, I have intermitted the pursuit. The intensity of thought, and the number of minute experiments with light and figure, have made me so nervous and feverish that I cannot sleep as long as I ought and have been used to do; and the sleep which I have is made up of ideas so connected, and so little different from the operations of reason, that it does not afford me the due refreshment. I shall therefore take a week's respite, and make *Christabel* ready for the press.

A week later:

To Poole, March 23, 1801.

My opinion is this: that deep thinking is attainable only by a man of deep feeling, and all truth is a species of revelation. . . . It is *insolent* to *differ* from the public *opinion* in *opinion*, if it be only *opinion*. It is sticking up little *i by itself*, i against the whole alphabet. But one *word* with *meaning* in it is worth the whole alphabet together. Such is a sound argument, an incontrovertible fact.

This shows, at least, what an immense step Coleridge felt that he was taking. And he was right. To us, a Kantian Copernican step or a doctrine of the creative mind are so familiar that we may even wonder how men have ever failed to hit on them. But to a Coleridge, in whom Hartley's Associationism had been more than a theory, had been a clue to be passionately pursued through a labyrinth, richer in turns and wonders, if not more baffling, than those which other men wander in, the sudden vision of a new principle must have been staggering. If it had been merely arresting there would be no cause for surprise; a similar shock has in fact merely arrested a great number of minds since. To Coleridge's mobile and indefatigable intelligence the new revelation was chiefly an occasion for retracing what he had already learnt about the mind under the guidance of Hartley, Locke or Hume. I do not mean that he set to work to reinterpret them; he did in fact waste a great deal of energy in refuting them. But into the developing system of the new theory that grew out of these midnight feverish hours he carried over, sometimes without recognizing them, masses of valuable observation which he could hardly have made without the help of his earlier studies.

This is, I think, the important fact about Coleridge's conversion from Hartley to Kant. The two systems (or set of assumptions), violently opposed though they seemed to him, may each—to a Coleridge—be ways of surveying our mind. In the final theory what he had learned from each came together. A later inquirer, for whom materialist associationism and transcendental idealism are usually systems to be thought *of* rather than to be thought *with*, is not likely to learn so much either *through* or *about* either.

Mill, in those first dozen pages of his *Essay on Coleridge* (which are still the best introduction to him) points out that the two characteristic figures of English philosophy were Coleridge and Bentham —men as opposed in their intellectual outlook as they could be.

By Bentham, beyond all others, men have been led to ask themselves, in regard to any ancient or received opinion, Is it true? and by Coleridge, What is the meaning of it? The one took his stand *outside* the received opinion, and surveyed it as an entire stranger to it; the other looked at it from *within*, and endeavoured to see it with the eyes of a believer in it; to discover by what apparent facts it was at first suggested, and by what appearances it has ever since been rendered continually credible—has seemed, to a succession of persons, to be a faithful interpretation of their experience. (*Dissertations and Discussions*, I, 394).

Perhaps this account is more flattering to Coleridge than perfectly just. He was not always as tolerant as Mill suggests. Yet the spirit attributed to Coleridge is certainly the spirit in which we must try to read the more transcendental parts of Coleridge himself. However repugnant to our opinions they may seem, they are, I think, an indispensable *introduction* (from which we may disengage ourselves later) to his theory of criticism. If we wish to understand this theory, we shall be foolish if we ignore or dismiss them as moonshine. We had better try instead to reinterpret them, to find, to quote Mill again, 'some natural want or requirement of human nature which the doctrine in question is fitted to satisfy.' But that is to put the point in terms appropriate to a Benthamite, as Mill was.

They are terms which come naturally to me— writing here as a Benthamite also. To quote Mill again:

> Whoever could master the principles and combine the methods of both would possess the entire English philosophy of his age. Coleridge used to say that everyone is born either a Platonist or an Aristotelian: it may similarly be affirmed that every Englishman of the present day is by implication either a Benthamite or a Coleridgean; holds views of human affairs which can only be proved true on the principles either of Bentham or of Coleridge.

What Mill says is still true—though we might

change the labels again and say, 'is either a Materialist or an Idealist.' It may be argued that these two opposite-seeming types of outlook are complementary to one another: that, in the history of thought they have been dependent upon one another so that the death of one would lead by inanition to the death of the other; that as expiration is only one phase in breathing so the two philosophies in their endless antagonism are a necessary conjoint self-critical process. But, since to hold neither is to have no view to offer, exposition requires a temporary choice between them. I write then as a Materialist trying to interpret before you the utterances of an extreme Idealist and you, whatever you be by birth or training, Aristotelian or Platonist, Benthamite or Coleridgean, Materialist or Idealist, have to reinterpret my remarks again in your turn.

It comes to this: Coleridge's criticism is of a kind that requires us, if we are to study it seriously, to reconsider our most fundamental conceptions, our conceptions of man's being—the nature of his mind and its knowledge. It is a chief merit of Coleridge's work that it forces us to do this and it is no defect that he forces us to do so more evidently than other critics. Our aim is to understand his opinions, if we can, and in so doing to understand our own. Whether we agree or not with them is, in comparison, of no importance. This is not an easy aim, and it will be well, before proceeding, to recall another sentence from Mill:

"Were we to search among men's recorded thoughts
for the choicest manifestations of human imbecility and
prejudice, our specimens would be mostly taken from
their opinions of the opinions of one another."—(408.)

When Coleridge says of his projected theory that
it 'would supersede all the books of metaphysics,
and all the books of morals too,' we are entitled,
I would urge, to suppose him not to be indulging
in hyperbole, but to be speaking of an achieved and
examined, though unrecorded, design. In what
view of morals and metaphysics could a theory of
Poetry replace them? This is a serious question
to which an answer would necessarily be long—
longer than this book; but, if words to explain
the matter to others are not required, an active
mind in a clear hour could cover most of it. I
hope, with what follows, to suggest that the problems
and methods of metaphysics and morals which
Coleridge's theory of poetry could supersede are
in fact those that have most exercised most
philosophers; and that they would be superseded
not by being taken into the theory and there solved
but by being shown to be, as problems, artificial,
and, as methods, inadequate. In much that
Coleridge wrote later (especially in *Biographia
Literaria,* 1816) he gives an opposite impression.
He seems to be merely re-formulating old problems.
What he gives becomes, beyond any disguise,[1] 'a

[1] Later the disguise recommended became *Philology*, rather than
the theory of Poetry. Derwent at Cambridge is advised to pursue
his studies " under the guidance and in the light of *Philology*, in that

system of morals and politics'. But by then he had been for years using a language borrowed from metaphysicians, and he was writing, we may suspect, as much from a memory of his thinking during this first creative period as from a renewed 'act of contemplation'.

To catch and record these 'realizing acts of intuition' he needed constructions. He took them mostly from his reading in Kant and Schelling, and with them he took in also very much that did not belong to his purpose, the development of the theory of poetry. What I shall try to do, so far as I can, is to use Coleridge's metaphysical machinery *as* machinery, disregarding the undeniable fact that Coleridge himself so often took it to be much more. I shall take his constructions, that is, as 'concepts of the understanding' [1] (to use his terminology) and use them, not as doctrines to be accepted, refuted or corrected (however great the temptations) but as instruments with which to explore the nature of poetry. Only later (in Chapter VII) shall I

original and noblest sense of the term, in which it *implies* and is the most *human*, practical and fructifying Form, and (what is of no small moment in the present state of society) the most popular *Disguise*, of Logic and Psychology—without which what is man? (The last five words I write with the line ' Without black velvet Breeches what is man? ' running in my head.) "

How far away from this are current senses of Philology!

[1] " And it may be that one secret of Coleridge's own influence on educators and logicians during the middle of the nineteenth century lay in the sense of freedom and potential control that he conveyed indirectly, by relegating the concepts of the understanding to the order of tools, shaped by and subservient to powers that more adequately expressed the ' total man '."—Snyder, *Coleridge on Logic and Learning*, p. 13.

attempt to reduce them from such concepts to the 'fact of mind' from which they come.

To keep this purpose steadily in sight is difficult. A guiding image may be of assistance. What we have to think of throughout our manipulation of these intricate treacherous abstract machines, is not the Highgate spell-binder, nor the voice that disputes through the central chapters of *Biographia Literaria*, but the young man sitting in his room at Greta Hall looking out on those views which he is never tired of describing to his correspondents ('O the perpetual forms of Borrowdale') and 'thinking with intense energy'.

"There is a deep blue cloud over the heavens; the lake, and the vale, and the mountains are all in darkness; only the *summits* of all the mountains in long ridges, covered with snow, are bright to a dazzling excess."

CHAPTER II

But if there be, or ever were, one such,
It's past the size of dreaming: nature wants stuff
To vie strange forms with fancy: yet to imagine
An Antony were nature's peace 'gainst fancy
Condemning shadows quite.

Antony and Cleopatra, V, ii.

IN the closing paragraph of Chapter iv of *Biographia*, one of the many places where Coleridge begins his explanation of 'the seminal principle' of imagination, he invokes the example of Hooker—"the judicious author" who "though he wrote for men of learning in a learned age, saw nevertheless reason to anticipate and guard against 'complaints of obscurity' as often as he was about to trace his subject 'to the highest well-spring and fountain'". The conception of the mind from which Coleridge drew his distinction between *Fancy* and *Imagination* did really deserve to be called 'the highest well-spring and fountain', and the danger of obscurity is not avoidable. But a part of it comes from other uses of the key terms, and this part, at least we may take measures against.

Distinctions marked by these terms were, of course, not new in the world when Coleridge took the problem up and, since his time, several senses of both words have been current which are not in origin or in effect the same as his. These, inter-

23

lacing, make a fog which may be dissipated most conveniently by examining a few specimens of other senses before turning to the exposition of his.

First we may take a wide, indefinite sense, which is also the most ancient: *imagination* contrasted with *imitation* (if we take imitation as mere copying, a mere reproduction, as close as the medium will permit, of what has been seen or known in some way). Imagination, in this sense, goes beyond, outdoes reproduction to present to the mind what has not been and cannot be known. I may take my example from Longinus, though my use of it does not adequately represent his view:

> Wherefore, not even the whole universe can suffice the reaches of man's thought and contemplation, but oftentimes his *imagination oversteps the bounds of space*, so that if we survey our life on every side, how greatness and beauty and eminence have everywhere the prerogative, we shall straightway perceive the end for which we were created (*On the Sublime*, xxxv).

Imagination here is the extrapolation of the known, in the interests of admiration.

> Hence it is that we are led by nature to admire, not our little rivers, for all their purity and homely uses, so much as Nile and Rhine and Danube, and, beyond all, the sea.[1]

The only link, and it is slight enough, between this and the Coleridgean Imagination is in the

[1] Here, and with Philostratus, Plotinus and Muratori below, I have used the translation by Mr E. F. Carritt in his very convenient and instructive collection, *Philosophies of Beauty*.

suggestion that the motive here is a passion—a yearning for expansion in the admiration.

This imagination is sharply unlike Coleridge's imagination in an important respect. The step from the familiar to 'greatness and beauty and eminence' seems to be along a simple line of exaggeration— bringing in nothing new, no modification or change of character; only increase in quantity. But there are other passages in Longinus in which this is not so, and he may be taken as anticipating much in Coleridge. Especially, when he speaks of a "power of choosing the most vital of the included elements and making them by a mutual superposition form as it were a single body" (x). But I am less concerned here with those who may have anticipated Coleridge than with some of his successors who have differed from him.

In Philostratus (said to be the earliest *locus* for the explicit use of the notion of imagination) a fundamental ambiguity may be found:

'Are you going to tell me,' said Thespesion, 'that your Pheidias and Praxiteles went up into heaven and took casts of the god's features and then fashioned them artistically, or had they any other guidance in their modelling?' 'Yes', said Apollonius, 'a guidance pregnant with wisdom.' 'What was it?', he said, 'surely you cannot mean anything but imitation?' 'Imagination,' replied the other, 'fashioned these works, a more cunning craftsman than imitation. For imitation will fashion what it has seen, but imagination goes on to what it has not seen, *which it will assume as the standard of the reality*' (*Life of Apollonius of Tyana*, vi, xix).

25

The last clause is translated by Saintsbury:

> supposing it according to the analogy of the Real

and comparison between the versions well brings out one deep opposition which haunts the whole subject: that between a *projective* outlook, which treats imagination's products as figment, and a *realist* outlook, which takes the imagination to be a means of apprehending reality.

The choice between the doctrine that we project values into nature and the doctrine that we discover them in her should be noticed as likely to show itself in *our* interpretations of several accounts of Imagination; but a discussion of it is best postponed (see Chapter VII) until the assumptions behind both views have been separated and examined. That we should be wrong in giving *either* interpretation to the remark of Philostratus seems likely if we note that he also says:

> If you are to fashion Athene, you must have in your mind strategy and counsel and the arts and how she sprang from Zeus himself.

The distinction is perhaps latent here, but it is not ready to be disengaged.

With Plotinus, there is the same opportunity for a two-fold interpretation, more explicitly given:

> This essence or character was not in the material, but it *was in the conceiving mind, even before it entered into the stone.* But it was in the artist not by virtue of his having eyes and hands, but by virtue of his imagination ($\tau \acute{\epsilon} \chi \nu \eta$). And this beauty, already *comprehended in his*

26

imagination, was far greater. For it went not out of him into the stone, but abode with him and gave birth to a lesser beauty. . . .

The arts do not merely copy the visible world but *ascend to the principles on which nature is built up*; and, further, many of their creations are original. For they certainly make good the defects of things, as having the source of beauty in themselves. Thus Pheidias did not use any visible model for his Zeus, but apprehended him as he would appear if he deigned to show himself to our eyes (V, viii, 1).

Plotinus is a source for much in Coleridge. Our later problem will be, in part: How should we give a detailed interpretation to the figurative language of the underlined phrases? There are a number of interpretations and Coleridge hesitates and changes between them. But this sense of *imagination* is certainly an ancestor of Coleridge's—of the same metaphysical family, with the deep duplicity that, covertly or openly, is constitutional in all the progeny of Plato.

After the Renaissance, more humdrum senses of *imagination* are common. We find it being used for *invention*, as with Dryden, the finding of material to be put into a work; for *imaging*, as with Addison, the formation of pictures in the mind's eye; and for any kind of thinking of absent or 'unreal' things. In this last use, as Bergson has remarked (*Les deux sources de la morale et de la religion*, p. 207), it has 'un sens plutôt négatif. On appelle imaginatives les représentations concrètes qui ne sont ni des perceptions ni des souvenirs.' Here and there we have, however, senses which come nearer to Coleridge's, and may more usefully be distinguished from it. Thus, for Peter Sterry,

> (The Imagination) this *first* and *highest* faculty of the *sensitive Soul* where it is in its *perfection*, is as ample as the *universal object* of *sense*, the whole *Corporeal world*. . . . It not only takes in and *enjoys* the *sensitive forms* of all the *objects* of *sense*, *uniting* and *varying* them according to its own pleasure, but also . . . it *espouseth* in itself the *spiritual* and *corporeal world* to each other, receiving the *impressions*, the *similitudes*, the *illapses* of the *invisible Glories* as the *Originals* into their *sensitive Image*, and . . . *heightening* the *sensitive Image* to a greatness and glory *above* itself by this communion with its invisible patterns (V. de S. Pinto, *Peter Sterry, Platonist and Puritan*, p. 103).

How these metaphors should be read is again the problem. Probably Sterry took his Plato more literally than Coleridge did, but it is hard to be sure, and *literal* is a deceiving word here, where metaphor is mounted upon metaphor like the motions of the heavenly bodies.

Later, a changed interest in truth turns what may seem a very similar view (equally Platonic) into more familiar and more easily discussed doctrine.

> The power or faculty of the mind which apprehends and recognizes sensible objects or, to speak more accurately, their images, is *the imagination or fancy*; which, being placed, as we hold, in the inferior part of the soul, we may conveniently call *Inferior Apprehension*. Our soul has another apprehension of things, which we call *Superior*, because it is placed in the superior,

reasonable and divine part, and which is commonly named *Understanding*. . . . The office of the imagination is not to inquire or know if things are true or false, but merely to apprehend them; it is the office of the understanding to know and to inquire if these are true or false. When we reflect or think, these two powers co-operate, the inferior supplying the superior with images or shadows of objects out of its store-house without fresh recourse to the senses (Muratori, *The Perfection of Italian Poetry*, 1706, xiv).

We may notice in this, as sharply different from what we shall find in Coleridge:

1. Imagination and fancy are not desynonymized.
2. There is a certain implied discrediting of the senses.
3. The notion of a storehouse of images or shadows of things, which, though Coleridge sometimes uses this figure of speech, does not belong to his theory.
4. Imagination is subordinate and has no concern with knowledge.

Muratori has other passages, however, which do point forward to parts of Coleridge's doctrine. He has a reference to "images formed by the imagination when, excited by some passion, it unites two simple and natural images and gives them a *shape and nature different from the representation of* the senses. In doing this, the imagination for the most part pictures lifeless things as alive." He instances the imagination of the lover: "His violent passion makes him, for example, conceive the company and caresses of his beloved to be bliss so rare and enviable that *he truly and naturally imagines all other beings, even grass and flowers, to burn and sigh for that felicity.* . . . This," Muratori explains, "is the delusion of a love-sick imagination, but the poet represents this delusion to others, as it was born in his imagination, to make them apprehend vividly the violence of his own passion."

When Muratori says, "the lover . . . *truly and naturally* imagines the grass to sigh for that felicity," should we take him as saying that the lover (or the poet as lover) really does imagine this as a genuine apprehension of the mind (mistaken or not) or as a conceit, a feigning designed to show or exercise his passion?[1]   Whether, if it is a genuine apprehension, it is mistaken or not, is a point we shall have to consider closely. *His* grass, *as he has imagined it*, does undoubtedly sigh; and we are not entitled to deny this on the ground that the grass *we* tread on and the cows munch does *not* sigh.[2] All turns here upon what 'grass' stands for. This question will be considered at some length later, in Chapter VII. It is important for its bearing upon the two doctrines mentioned above in connection with the translation of Philostratus. It is still more important because from differences in the procedure of poets here many of the most subtle and far-reaching changes in the tradition of poetry have

[1] As we read him one way or another the whole structure of his poem may be changed.   (See Chapter IX.)

[2] Then I asked: " does a firm perswasion that a Thing is so, make it so? "

Isaiah replied: " All poets believe that it does, & in ages of imagination this firm perswasion removed mountains; but many are not capable of a firm perswasion of any thing."—Blake, *The Marriage of Heaven and Hell.*

derived. And with these changes we have corresponding aberrations in criticism. Indeed to say, for example, that because the common grass does not sigh, the poet's may not, is all the argument behind many resolute misreadings.

These glances at some pre-Coleridgean speculations about imagination may be followed up by a brief examination of some recent attempts to appreciate what he did for us. They will help us to see where, in spite of Coleridge, current opinion is in this matter; and they raise a question which ought certainly to be examined early. I will begin with some remarks of Professor Lowes', for whose command of Coleridge material all students must have the deepest respect and admiration. From his conception of Coleridge's theory, however, I am obliged to dissent. In *The Road to Xanadu* (p. 103) he says:

> But I have long had the feeling, which this study has matured to a conviction, that Fancy and Imagination are not two powers at all, but one. The valid distinction which exists between them lies, not in the materials with which they operate, but in the degree of intensity of the operant power itself. Working at high tension the imaginative energy assimilates and transmutes; keyed low, the same energy aggregates and yokes together those images which at its highest pitch, it merges indissolubly into one.

Since an observable and definable difference between Fancy and Imagination is the central point of Coleridge's critical theory, it will evidently be well to examine this negative opinion closely.[1] We have to ask in what terms this rival psychological theory is framed. Some trouble here will be repaid, for this theory presents itself, more or less explicitly, in most discussions of the subject. It follows an obvious line of analogy, and we should be clear why this type of analogy is inadequate if we are to see the merits of more refined theories. The metaphor used here is that of an electrical furnace. Turn the current on at low tension and the elements are welded together: turn it on at higher tension and they are melted up and fused. It should be carefully noted that Professor Lowes holds that the materials operated with are the same, and that only the degree of the 'operant power' varies. But what are these materials?

Professor Lowes (following Coleridge in an unfortunate practice) calls them images. This is unfortunate, because the term *image* is ambiguous at a point at which precision is desirable. An

[1] We should compare with it *B. L.*, I, 60: " Repeated meditations led me first to suspect (and a more intimate analysis of the human faculties, their appropriate marks, functions, and effects matured my conjecture into full conviction), that fancy and imagination were two distinct and widely different faculties, instead of being, according to the general belief, either two names with one meaning, or, at furthest, the lower and higher degree of one and the same power." Professor Lowes has paid generous, discerning tribute to Coleridge as a psychologist, " Few human beings, I take it, have ever pondered more deeply than Coleridge the mysterious ' goings on ' of their own minds, and few who so pondered ever had, perhaps, such complex workings to explore, or such lynx-like intellect with which to track them " (*op. cit.*, 483). The chief division of such a psychologist—constituting the two eyes of his theory—surely deserves closer consideration.

image may be, for example, a visual image, a copy of a sensation; or it may be an idea, any event in the mind which represents something; or it may be a figure of speech, a double unit involving a comparison. Incidentally that so many writers are still content (Mr Wilson Knight is a recent example) to build up elaborate theories in terms so treacherous as this, suggests a need for more discipline in literary speculation.

The materials with which Professor Lowes' 'operant power' works, may, it seems, be any units of meaning. Any meanings whatsoever, he suggests, may, if the operant power is great enough, be assimilated. Let us test this upon any of Coleridge's examples:

> And like a lobster boyl'd the Morn
> From black to red began to turn.

This, from *Hudibras*, is Fancy (*Table Talk*, June 23, 1834). Professor Lowes' theory involves us in saying that, if the 'operant power' which here merely puts these units of meaning together had been working at higher tension, they would have been fused and merged indissolubly into one: that Butler's Morn would have become a Lobster boiling in a pot perhaps!

Surely it is evident that there are meanings which no operant power, however great, will fuse together, in a sane mind; as evident as the fact that no biologic pressure, however great, will make a whelk grow wings. Some meanings, thanks to their

C   33

structure under the conditions we summarize as 'poetic contemplation,' will grow together; others will not, under any conditions compatible with sanity. This is the firm ground of observation and experiment we set out from. When we introduce the inappropriate though handy metaphor of mental materials worked on by a hypothetic force, we leave it. The metaphor is sometimes convenient, but it will mislead us whenever we take it seriously. And Coleridge's theory must not be translated, for example, into a view that the step from Fancy to Imagination is across a critical point, like that between ice and water. His theory kept closer to the facts, and relied not upon popular analogies but upon an observable difference between instances of mental process.

This difference is not only observable but describable and of use in many branches of psychology. In fact his distinction is one of the few which have yet been made that are of use in comparing forms of growth and changes of structure in the mind. It is not a distinction introduced *ad hoc* for literary purposes. Professor Lowes has substituted for Coleridge's distinction—in terms of verifiably different modes of operation in the mind—another distinction much vaguer and less applicable. His distinction is in terms of *degrees* in a not further describable 'operant power'. But the only advantage in introducing degrees [1] is if we should be able to measure and compare them. Here we cannot do

---

[1] See *Basic Rules of Reason*, pp. 121–124.

this. And if, in attempting to do so, we look more closely into the observable relations between the units of meaning in Coleridge's cases of Fancy and Imagination, we shall find ourselves step by step reinstating his distinction; we shall be, in fact, going through the process of rediscovering it. I conclude that—unless the rival theory is taken to be about elements not known to psychology (or in any other way at present observable or identifiable) and about their transformation by a power that psychology finds equally useless—it is no more than an initial speculation of the kind from which Coleridge set out. But the ground for this will not appear until Coleridge's distinction has been expounded (Chapter I-V).

In support of his opinion Professor Lowes quotes Professor Lascelles Abercrombie:

> Now the faculty of Fancy does not exist: it is one of Coleridge's chimeras,[1] of which he kept a whole stable. Fancy is nothing but a degree of imagination; and the degree of it concerns, not the quality of the imagery, but the quality and force of the emotion symbolized by the imagery (*The Idea of Great Poetry*, p. 58).

Every set of sentences has, as it were, an invisible load mark—like those on railway trucks—telling

---

[1] "But alas ! The halls of old philosophy have been so long deserted, that we circle them at shy distance as the haunt of phantoms and chimeras. The sacred grove of Academus is holden in like regard with the unfoodful trees in the shadowy world of Maro that had a dream attached to every leaf. The very terms of ancient wisdom are worn out, or (far worse !) stamped on baser metal: and whoever should have the hardihood to reproclaim its solemn truths must commence with a glossary."—*The Statesman's Manual*.

you how much weight you can put on them; and since these remarks contain at least a very familiar sniff at Coleridge as a psychologist it will be permissible to inquire what else they carry. The words that take the strain are *quality* and *emotion* and *symbolized*, evidently. Let us see what they mean here. All sorts of qualities, of course, are used in psychology (red, sweet, vivid, pleasurable, gay, are specimens), but none that I know of is general enough to fit in here. Pondering the sentence, we seem to have two choices only. Either *quality* here is not a psychologically descriptive term at all and is only being used in commendation—as the draper uses it in, 'Very best quality, Madam!' Or, if psychological, it is equivalent to 'some undefined respect'. I take Professor Abercrombie therefore to be perhaps saying this: "The degree of the imagination concerns, not some undefined respect of the imagery, but some undefined respect and force of the emotion symbolized by the imagery." It is hard though to see how anyone could be so confident about anything like this. But let us look now at *emotion*.

A good general prescription whenever we meet with this word in critical prose, is to try replacing it with *commotion*—a word which very commonly will have the same *sense* with different emotive accompaniments. *Emotion* has a range of stricter senses in psychology, and it may be that Professor Abercrombie is using one of them; but I cannot think he is; he would have found a more adequate

36

description than 'quality and force'. The opposition too, between the imagery which *symbolizes* and the emotion that is symbolized misleads inquiry. Ask how the one does symbolize the other—what their relations must be for this to happen—and the idleness of this separation of them is soon confessed. It is the meaning of the imagery (or the imagery as carrying meaning) that the poet is concerned with. Coleridge's distinction is between different structures of these meanings, a distinction finer and more exact than terms such as 'quality', 'force', 'intensity', 'richness', 'range' and 'depth' can convey.

Here again, as with Professor Lowes, the notion of degree beclouds the whole matter. Indeed the difficulty of applying considerations of degree in psychology, except, as it were, to the skin of the subject, to the most elementary characters of the sensations, and to a few other points, is familiar and notorious. Whoever tries, as Coleridge did, to think persistently and in detail about the operations of the mind, discovers quickly how impossible it is to order its doings by degrees of some single factor or power. But in the course of this detailed thinking Coleridge became a trained student—read in the subject and accustomed to the peculiar mixture of abstract speculation with experiment and introspection that it entails. It is to be expected then that what he found to say after his inquiries will not be understood by those without a similar training. This is true of all special studies. Psychology, however, is peculiar in that those who are not students in it feel ready so often to correct those who were.

I can point this observation with the example of Pater. Here is his anticipation of the pronouncements we have just examined:

"Some English critics at the beginning of the present century had a great deal to say concerning a distinction, of much importance, as they thought, in the true estimate of poetry, between the Fancy, and another more powerful faculty—the Imagination. This metaphysical distinction borrowed originally from the writings of German philosophers, and perhaps not always clearly apprehended by those who talked of it, involved a far deeper and more vital distinction, with which indeed all true criticism more or less directly has to do, the distinction, namely, between higher and lower degrees of intensity in the poet's perception of his subject, and in his concentration of himself on his work. Of those who dwelt upon the metaphysical distinction between the Fancy and the Imagination, it was Wordsworth who made the most of it, assuming it as the basis for the final classification of his poetical writings. . . ." (*Appreciations*, Essay on Wordsworth, p. 37).

It is worth remarking that the *tone* of critical writing (with the best writers) changes in the last third of the nineteenth century. Coleridge, Wordsworth, Shelley, Peacock, Hazlitt . . . on the whole address their readers as their equals. With Pater we have the beginning of that precarious clinging to a privileged position which has since become so familiar. We have since had intellectual snobs, spiritual snobs, sensibility-snobs, taste-snobs . . .

among our prominent critics far more often than candid inquirers.

And with this came a flagging, a defeatist faintness of enterprise in the thinking. The more one reads Pater the more one must admire him for the suppleness (not subtlety) and variety of his thought, but the less can one respect the intentions, the design, the scope within which so much intelligence and sensitiveness were usually restricted. In comparison with Wordsworth, Coleridge, or Shelley, the complacency of his phrasing is striking. In this passage we can note: a patronizing (self-protective) tone, 'of much importance as they thought'; an airy omniscience (equally self-protective) 'borrowed originally from the writings of German philosophers and perhaps not always clearly apprehended by those who talked of it'; and a careful ambiguity—'it was Wordsworth who made the most of it'—with reference to a classification thought by everyone since to be absurd, and happily compared by 'Q' to the Oxford shop-front inscribed UNIVERSITY PORK AND FAMILY BUTCHER.

But it is more important for our purposes to note what Pater makes of Coleridge's distinction. He earnestly replaces it with what? 'A far deeper and more vital distinction. . . . The distinction between higher and lower degrees of intensity *in the poet's perception of his subject* and *in his concentration of himself upon his work.*' Let us consider both these rather closely.

First this 'intensity of the poet's perception of his

39

subject'. Since Pater is sweeping away the work of exact thinkers and careful writers, it is legitimate to question him strictly. We can leave aside the nebulous confusion brought in with *subject*. We shall have enough with *intensity of perception*. How then do perceptions differ in intensity? The answer is that, unless we are using the words very loosely, they do not. The motives governing a perception may be said to vary in intensity; so can some of the effects of the perception.[1] But the perception itself cannot. What is perceived may be said to be more or less intense—a brighter or dimmer light, for example. The effort made in attention may be described as greater or less, and such a description may be given some intelligible interpretation, but the perception itself, the act or event of perceiving, though it may vary in a score of other ways, escapes any measure of intensity. We can perceive more or less clearly, with more or less detail, more or less precision, ease, coherence, certainty, discrimination . . . all these descriptions can be interpreted (they are more complex than they seem) and instances of such perceptions can be tested. But

[1] What may, in a descriptive context, be described as 'intensity of perception' may be illustrated by the following passage from Mrs Woolf's *To the Lighthouse*, p. 41: "Suddenly, as if the movement of his hand had released it, the load of her accumulated impressions of him tilted up, and down poured in a ponderous avalanche all she felt about him. That was one sensation. Then up rose in a fume the essence of his being. That was another. She felt herself transfixed by the intensity of her perception; it was his severity; his goodness." It will be observed that it is the accompanying and resultant *feelings* here that are intense. 'Intense perception' is, of course, an unobjectionable phrase, except in technical contexts.

40

we cannot measure the intensity of perceptions, because, if we separate a perception from its causes and consequences, its conditions and its repercussions, at all carefully, we can give no interpretation to its intensity.

If we do not make this separation it tends to become a name for all that may be going on in the mind, which brings us to Pater's second proposed scale—degrees of the poet's 'concentration of himself on his work'. Concentration of himself. What is *himself* here? How are we to estimate this? If we try, it becomes *either* a remark worthy of a School-master's Report ('finds difficulty in concentrating on his work') *or*, as we go into the questions that come up, distinguishing between the various modes of combination of different distinguishable types of mental activity, we find once again that we are repeating Coleridge's work. "The poet, described in ideal perfection, brings the whole soul of man into activity, with the subordination of its faculties to one another according to their relative worth and dignity . . ." (*Biographia Literaria*, II, p. 12). We discover, comparing Pater and Coleridge, that Pater's is amateur's work, mere nugatory verbiage—empty, rootless and backgroundless postulation—unless we put into it just that very piece of patient laborious analysis that it pretends so airily to dismiss or surpass.

A fair parallel to this queer but not unrepresenta-tive incident in criticism would be this. Suppose a schoolboy, bored with the detail of chemistry, to write: "Certain people calling themselves chemists have lately had a great deal to say concerning a distinction, of much importance as they thought . . . between inorganic and organic substances. This technical distinction, borrowed originally from Plato, and perhaps not always clearly apprehended by those who talked of it, involves a far deeper and more vital distinction, with which indeed all true chemistry more or less directly has to do, the distinction, namely, between higher and lower degrees of livingness of things."

Coleridge's life work in the theory of criticism was given to providing an improved basis in psychology, by which such easy remarks (which he no less than Pater, could produce without thinking a minute) could be given detailed and discussable meaning. I have lingered with Pater's unlucky paragraph because the spirit which animates it is by no means defunct. It is still powerful in English criticism. It has had such honoured and influential vehicles as Professor Mackail: "But when he goes beyond a saying like this ('Poetry is the best words in the best order') he becomes, like others who have made attempts to define poetry, confused and unreal. . . . His general ideas are nebulous, he becomes intoxicated with his own rhetoric and dialectic." Any reader who is interested in Coleridge will know of more recent examples. I hope to show that Coleridge was aware of, and actively at work on, problems and possibilities in the poetic and the ordinary consciousness which have not been surmised by later critics who doubt the value of his theories so easily; to show too that the exploration of these possibilities is only at its beginning; and that Coleridge succeeded in bringing his suggestions to a point from which, with a little care and pertinacity they can be taken on to become a new science.

CHAPTER III

THE COALESCENCE OF SUBJECT AND OBJECT

We imagine ourselves discoverers, and that we have struck a light, when, in reality, at most, we have but snuffed a candle.—*Anima Poetae.*

Nihil novum, vel inauditum audemus, tho' as every man has a force of his own, without being more or less than a man, so is every true Philosopher an original.—*Letter to J. Gooden, Jan.* 14, 1820.

In beginning now to expound Coleridge's theory of the Imagination, I propose to start where he himself in the *Biographia* (after all his endless preliminaries, warnings and preparations) really started: that is, with a theory of the act of knowledge, or of consciousness, or, as he called it, 'the coincidence or coalescence of an OBJECT with a SUBJECT'.

Upon how we understand these two terms and how we understand this *coalescence* of the two, a large part of our understanding of Coleridge's theory will depend.

And here at once comes up a practical difficulty. Coleridge insists (*B. L.*, I, p. 172) that Philosophy uses what he calls the INNER SENSE and that therefore it cannot 'like geometry, appropriate to every construction a correspondent *outward* intuition'.

For example, a geometer can think of a line. Then if he wishes he can draw one (or image one). The stroke is not the line itself (having length without breadth) but it satisfactorily images the

44

line (as a mathematical line) and it is 'an efficient
mean to excite every imagination to the intuition
of it'.

But where operations and acts of the inner sense
are concerned matters are not so easy. We are all
practised in thinking of lines—we are not all equally
practised in using the INNER SENSE:

> One man's consciousness extends only to the pleasant
> or unpleasant sensations caused in him by external
> impressions; another enlarges his inner sense to a
> consciousness of forms and quantity; a third in addition
> to the image is conscious of the conception or notion
> of the thing; a fourth attains to a notion of his notions—
> he reflects upon his own reflections; and thus we may
> say without impropriety that the one possesses more
> or less inner sense than the other. This more or less
> betrays already that philosophy in its first principles
> must have a practical or moral, as well as a theoretical
> or speculative side (*B. L.*, I, 172).

As Blake put it, 'A fool sees not the same tree
that a wise man sees.'

Coleridge supposes that these successive levels, as
it were, of the operation of the INNER SENSE are
stages that can be attained—with practice—by the
right people; that from notions of our notions we
can go on to an INNER SENSE of the act of notioning,
of the acts of choosing among our notions and
framing them, comparing them and so on, and he
begins his philosophy with a certain act of contemplation, a *realizing intuition* which brings into
existence what he calls 'the first postulate of
philosophy' *an instrument to be used in his later de-*

scriptions (as a geometer may postulate a construction of lines as an instrument to be used in geometry).

But this initial act of contemplation is not mere theoretical apprehension such as can be instigated by words in anyone who is acquainted with a language. Nor is it possible for everyone:

> To an Esquimau or New Zealander our most popular philosophy would be wholly unintelligible. The sense, the inward organ for it, is not yet born in him. So is there many a one among us, yes, and some who think themselves philosophers too, to whom the philosophic organ is entirely wanting. To such a man philosophy is a mere play of words and notions, like a theory of music to the deaf, or like the geometry of light to the blind. The connection of the parts and their logical dependencies may be seen and remembered; but the whole is groundless and hollow, unsustained by living contact, unaccompanied with any realizing intuition which exists by and in the act that affirms its existence, which is known, because it is, and is, because it is known. The words of Plotinus, in the assumed person of nature, hold good of the philosophic energy. . . . With me the act of contemplation makes the thing contemplated, as the geometricians contemplating describe lines correspondent; but I am not describing lines, but simply contemplating, the representative forms of things rise up into existence (*B. L.*, I, p. 173).

What he is asking us to do is to perform for ourselves an act of contemplation, of *realizing intuition*, at the same time and in the same act becoming aware by the INNER SENSE of what we are doing.

Here is the postulate:

The postulate of philosophy and at the same time the test of philosophic capacity, is no other than the heaven-descended KNOW THYSELF (E coelo descendit, Γνῶθι σεαυτόν). And this at once practically and speculatively. For as philosophy is neither a science of the reason or understanding only, nor merely a science of morals, but the science of BEING altogether, its primary ground can be neither merely speculative, nor merely practical, but both in one. All knowledge rests on the coincidence of an object with a subject.

It will be noticed that Coleridge deliberately makes this postulate seem *arbitrary*. It is an act of the will, a direction of the *inner sense*, a mode of action, or of being, at the same time that it is a mode of knowing. It is that activity of the mind in which knowing and doing and making and being are least to be distinguished.

In order to be able to make this postulate (or to use it) we must have sufficiently developed our inner sense. We must be more than merely aware, we must be aware of our awareness, and of the form and mode of operation of our awareness. The rest of his philosophy is a verbal machine for exhibiting what the exercise of this postulate or this act of contemplation yielded. (As the geometer's drawn diagrams and written theorems are a machine for exhibiting his acts of *realizing intuition*.) We must study it *as a machine*—with a recognition that in the nature of the case it must be a very inefficient machine—useful only so far as it helps us to go through the same *realizing intuitions*.

At this point I had better raise and meet—if I can—an objection. Someone will say, "But this is only *introspection* glorified into a method of research. And introspection is notoriously misleading. The tendency of psychology, as psychology becomes a science, is to depose it and reduce its claims." The right answer to which is, I think, this: that *introspection* (the seemingly direct inspection by the mind of the mind's own processes) is discredited, and rightly, as a means of settling matters *not* within the scope of direct inspection (*e.g.* whether colour-contrast effects arise in the retina or farther back in the head; how we locate sounds; or whether the eye follows a smooth line more easily than a jagged one) but that there still remains a field in which introspection is not only a possible but an indispensable source of information, and that all modes of systematic inquiry use at some point comparisons whose method is nothing but introspection.

But there is a subtler question than this to be noticed. It may be said that introspection only sees what it expects to see—the framework of assumptions through which it is made. We must reply that this by itself is something, is much, is all we can ask, and all we need. Definitive final results are not to be hoped for in these matters. What we want are possible, useful hypotheses, ways of conceiving the mind that may help us in living.

Self-knowledge is obviously an unusually dangerous phrase—even among philosophical phrases. The mere exercise of introspection, the effort to make

out what we are doing as we think, the detection of
our assumptions, the tracking down of obscure
motives, the observation of components in consciousness that are not ordinarily attended to, and so on,
is not to be confused either with the act which
supplies Coleridge's initial postulate—the realizing
intuition—*or* with the mode of self-creation which
Coleridge is going on to use in dividing the
Imagination from the Fancy. Introspection is
clearly not in itself Imagination: it supplies us as
a rule with *notions* only, not with a fresh development
of our selves. But we are concerned at present only
with Coleridge's initial postulate. His Γνῶθι σεαυτόν
is a technique for making certain assumptions—
living them in order thereby to discover what it is
we are making. As we have seen, Coleridge's theory
of knowing treats knowing as a kind of making,
i.e. the bringing into being of what is known. By
itself, it makes no discoveries except in the sense of
discovering what it has made.

One feature of Coleridge's thinking needs to be
pointed out early. It is not peculiar to him, though
the disorder in his exposition sometimes makes this
feature seem specially obtrusive. *After* he has stated
some principle (or objection) in a subtle form, with
a meaning that no one with a fairly open and
curious mind can doubt would be worth exploring,
he is apt to repeat something like it, in similar words,
but fairly evidently with a meaning by no means
the same.

For example, *here* he has taken Γνῶθι σεαυτόν as

D   49

the first postulate of philosophy—and with an implication that the self that has to be known is a
self that is created in the act of endeavouring to
know it. "The inner sense," he says, "has its
direction determined for the greater part by an act
of freedom" (*B. L.*, i, p. 172). This was in 1817.

Fifteen years later he writes as follows:

> Γνῶθι σεαυτόν!—and is this the prime
> And heaven-sprung maxim of the olden time!—
> Say canst thou make thyself? Learn first that trade:—
> Haply thou may'st know what thyself has't made.
> What has't thou, Man, that thou dar'st call thine own?
> What is there in thee, Man, that may be known?
> Dark fluxion, all unfixable by thought,
> A Phantom dim of past and future wrought,
> Vain sister of the worm,—life, death, soul, clod,
> Ignore thyself and seek to know thy God!

A passage, unless I mistake, streaked through, if
read dramatically, with the less familiar veins of
Coleridge's best poetry. Read it, not dramatically,
but for the *prose-sense* and for the feelings towards
the doctrines it then presents (scorn, timidity and
bafflement) and it is, in almost similar words,
directly contrary to the former doctrine. For the
earlier Γνῶθι σεαυτόν had promised that in the
effort to know ourselves we might in a real sense
make ourselves—and these verses seem almost to
spit scorn on the endeavour. There is a long and
terrible chapter of Coleridge's biography to be read
between them.

In the earlier doctrine there is a sense in which

to seek to know God may be interpreted as the safest method of knowing oneself. But that was with an altogether different sense for the words 'seek to know thy God', a sense which the later verses, unless I misread them,[1] seem to forget or deny. And with this change come other changes in the senses of 'self' and 'thought'.

It may seem that—imitating Coleridge in the respects in which it is most easy to imitate him— I have forgotten that I proposed to begin with *the coalescence of the Subject and the Object*. But the postulate Γνῶθι σεαυτόν is only this coalescence in other words. Coleridge's *Subject* is the Self or the Intelligence, the sentient knowing Mind; his *Object* is Nature, what is known by the mind in the act of knowing. The coalescence of the two is that knowing (making, being) activity we have been considering.

We need here both a free eye and a light hand. We have to make certain distinctions and, while making them, never to forget that we make them for certain purposes only, and that we can unmake them and *must do so* for other purposes. "While I am attempting to explain this intimate coalition, I must suppose it dissolved," said Coleridge. A separated Subject and Object cannot be put together again without the distinction between them lapsing. These distinctions were made only

[1] It is very possible, though, that Coleridge has just been stung by Pope, in which case it is rather 'the monstrous puerilities of CONDILLAC and CONDORCET' that are being attacked.

for conveniences of abstract theory and of practical action. The scope of the conveniences is wide, so wide that the distinctions—between the self that knows, its knowing, its knowledge and what it knows—may seem inevitable, established in their own right as part of the order of existence. But for other purposes, as when our knowing *in the act of the realizing intuition* is developing itself, they are not ruling. "There is here no first, and no second; both are coinstantaneous and one." The distinctions are not then being used by the Subject-Object, nor are they useful to us in describing its act (or being)— any more than when a plant is growing we can distinguish what grows, its growing, the growledge and what is grown. Though Coleridge says (*B. L.*, I, p. 180), "To know is in its very essence a verb active", he is often in fact paralleling knowing with growing: "the *rules* of the IMAGINATION are themselves the very powers of growth and production' (*B. L.*, II, p. 65). His clearest statement, in a very important passage in *The Statesman's Manual* (Appendix B) is in these terms:

Further, and with particular reference to that un-divided reason, neither merely speculative or merely practical, but both in one . . . I seem to myself to behold in the quiet objects on which I am gazing, more than an arbitrary illustration, more than a mere *simile*, the work of my own fancy. I feel an awe, as if there were before my eyes the same power as that of the reason—the same power in a lower dignity, and there-fore a symbol established in the truth of things. I feel it alike, whether I contemplate a single tree or flower, or meditate on vegetation throughout the world, as one of the great organs of the life of nature. Lo![1]— with the rising sun it commences its outward life and enters into open communion with all the elements, at once assimilating them to itself and to each other. . . . Lo!—how upholding the ceaseless plastic motion of the parts in the profoundest rest of the whole it becomes the visible *organismus* of the entire silent or elementary life of nature.

That in the *products* of knowing we later have occasion to distinguish Subject from Object does not entail their separation in the *process*. The senses of the words change as our discussion moves from the one to the other. We need to take them apart to explain them and to divide off the sphere of natural science (including physiology). We need to take them together to explore the act of knowing by means of the inner sense, and to divide off the sphere of what may be called pure psychology. But since the assumptions introduced for the convenience of these different purposes are different (and thus the terms used in the two spheres have different senses) we cannot bring them together without a mediating method of interpretation. There is thus a gap left between natural science and psychology which thought has not yet succeeded

[1] The remainder of the paragraph might properly form the conclusion of a disquisition on the spirit, as suggested by meditative observation of natural objects, and of our own thoughts and impulses without reference to any theological dogma, or any religious obligation to receive it as a revealed truth, but traced to the law of the dependence of the particular on the universal, the first being the organ of the second, as the lungs in relation to the atmosphere, the eye to light . . . and the like.—*Coleridge's Footnote.*

in bridging. Because, we may conjecture, it is a gap introduced only by our mode of formulating the problem.

Coleridge made acute remarks in several places about the pernicious effect of the 'despotism of the eye' under which 'we are restless because invisible things are not the objects of vision'. "Metaphysical systems, for the most part, become popular not for their truth, but in proportion as they attribute to causes a susceptibility of being seen, if only our visual organs were sufficiently powerful." But a diagrammatic presentation of Coleridge's philosophical position, and its difficulties, will, I hope, here economize exposition, and, with this warning, need not mislead. It is no more than

Subject	'Mind'
↓	↑
Aware of (perceiving)	Brain
↓	↑
Object	Receptor (*e.g.* eye)
(The apparition of a man)	↑
	Light waves
	↑
	Agitations in some physical system

a compact *aide mémoire*. Let us take what has become a 'common-sense' view of perception—it is really the view of popular science—and place it on the Right-hand side of our diagram, with a gap to divide it from a psychological view of perception on the Left in which a Conscious Subject is aware of an Object, say a man.

54

For Coleridge, of course, there is no Right-hand side to the picture; it is absorbed into the Object in the Left-hand division which contains all that is known. What I have there labelled the 'apparition of a man' is not, for Coleridge, an apparition but the man himself. The Object is not 'a something without . . . which occasions the objects of their perceptions' but the man himself. "It is the table itself, which the man of common-sense believes himself to see—not the phantom of a table, from which he may argumentatively deduce the reality of a table which he does not see" (*B. L.*, I, 179). And the Subject for Coleridge is equally not a hypothetical abstraction, a conscious ego about which nothing can be known; but it is an Act of knowing— 'a realizing intuition'. It is 'a subject which becomes a subject by the act of constructing itself objectively to itself; but which never is an object except for itself, and only so far as by the very same act it becomes a subject' (*B. L.*, I, 183).

The coalescence of the Subject and the Object in the act of knowing is a difficult doctrine—partly because it needs practising, partly because other senses of *Subject* and *Object* (and still more of *subjective* and *objective*) are so easily confused with these.

For example, we may take *objective* as 'outside and independent of my mind or any mind,' which would make nonsense of the doctrine. Or we may take *subjective* as 'dependent upon wishes, feelings, state of expectation, prior conceptions, and so on,' which again is not Coleridge's sense here. And we are likely to be more familiar with these senses—through discussions as to whether Beauty, for example, is subjective or objective.

Another distinction for which *subjective* and *objective* are used is also likely to be confused into the problem. Feelings, desires, pain-pleasure (the affective—volitional aspects of consciousness) may be opposed as subjective, to sensations, images, ideas, conceptions (cognitive aspects of consciousness) presentations which seem to stand *over against* a conscious subject. These appear to be offered to contemplation in a way in which desires, for example, are not. This again is *not* Coleridge's distinction. It turns upon a piece of speculative psychological mythology that he does not use. In his best analyses he transposes feelings, thoughts, ideas, desires, images and passions with a freedom which descriptive psychology has only recently regained. He treats all these elements in the psychological inventory. as forms of the activity of the mind—different, of course, and with different functions—but not to be set over against one another in two groups either as products to be opposed to the processes which bring them into being, or as presentations to be set against the reverberations they arouse and which shift them about.

His subject-object machinery introduces no such split between the ingredients of the mind. It is for him an instrument for noting, and insisting, that nothing of which we are in any way conscious is

56

given to the mind. Into the simplest seeming 'datum' a constructing, forming activity from the mind has entered. And the perceiving and the forming are the same. The subject (the self) has gone into what it perceives, and what it perceives is, in this sense, itself. So the object becomes the subject and the subject the object. And as, to understand what Coleridge is saying, we must not take the object as something given to us; so equally we must not take the subject to be a mere empty formless void out of which all things mysteriously and ceaselessly rush to become everything we know. The subject is what it is through the objects it has been.

> Hard task to analyse a soul, in which,
> Not only general habits and desires,
> But each most obvious and particular thought,
> Not in a mystical, and idle sense,
> But in the words of reason deeply weighed
> Hath no beginning. (*Prelude*, II, 232.)

And here Coleridge's separation of a Primary from a Secondary Imagination may be considered. The celebrated closing paragraphs of the first volume of *Biographia* are as follows:

The primary IMAGINATION I hold to be the living Power and prime Agent of all human Perception, and as a repetition in the finite mind of the eternal act of creation in the infinite I AM. The secondary Imagination I consider as an echo of the former, co-existing with the conscious will, yet still as identical with the primary in the *kind* of its operation. It dissolves, diffuses, dissipates, in order to recreate; or where this process is rendered impossible, yet still at all events it struggles to idealize and to unify. It is essentially *vital*, even as all objects (*as* objects) are essentially fixed and dead.

FANCY, on the contrary, has no other counters to play with, but fixities and definites. The Fancy is indeed no other than a mode of Memory emancipated from the order of time and space; while it is blended with, and modified by that empirical phenomenon of the will, which we express by the word CHOICE. But equally with the ordinary memory the Fancy must receive all its materials ready made from the law of association.

The Primary Imagination is normal perception that produces the usual world of the senses,

> That inanimate cold world allowed
> To the poor loveless ever-anxious crowd

the world of motor-buses, beef-steaks, and acquaintances, the framework of things and events within which we maintain our everyday existence, the world of the routine satisfaction of our minimum exigences. The Secondary Imagination, re-forming this world, gives us not only poetry—in the limited sense in which literary critics concern themselves with it—but every aspect of the routine world in which it is invested with other values than these necessary for our bare continuance as living beings: all objects for which we can feel love, awe, admiration; every quality beyond the account of physics, chemistry and the physiology of sense-perception, nutrition, reproduction and locomotion; every awareness for which a civilized life is preferred by us to an uncivilized. All the supernumerary perceptions which support civilized life are the product of the Secondary Imagination; and, though the processes by which they are created are best studied in words—in the highest examples, in poetry —the rest of the fabric of the world of values is of the same origin. Thus, that there should be a connection between poetry and the ordering of life should not surprise. "If men will impartially, and not asquint, look toward the offices and function of a poet, they will easily conclude to themselves the impossibility of any man's being a great poet without being first a good man" (Ben Jonson's Dedication to *Volpone*, quoted by Coleridge in *Omniana*, 126).

Against both Primary and Secondary Imagination is set Fancy—which collects and re-arranges, without re-making them, units of meaning already constituted by Imagination. In Imagination the mind is growing; in Fancy it is merely reassembling products of its past creation, stereotyped as objects and obeying, as such 'fixities and definities', the laws of Hartley's Association. The passage from the conception of the mind's doings as Fancy to that of the creative Imagination is the passage from Hartley to Kant.

But it is not hard to see in the stress which he laid on this distinction a reflection of Coleridge's peculiar fate. The mind is not always, alas, a self-realizing activity (according to Locke, it does not always 'think'). In Dejection it loses self-activity,

59

the 'genial spirits fail'; it relapses into the
condition of a 'lazy looker-on'. Genius was 'the
power of doing something new'. It implied 'an
unusual intensity of the modifying power', and
was sharply opposed to talent. Even with 'the
king of the men of talent', 'you might not im-
properly write on his forehead, "Warehouse to
let!"' (*Table Talk*, April 27, 1823). Wordsworth
thought Coleridge even more remarkable for his
talent than for his genius. Hence the importance
for Coleridge (who knew more than most men what
misery lay in being unable to work the miracle)
of the power to shoot one's being through earth,
air and sea. The contrast between living power
and lifeless mechanism was no abstract matter with
him, but a daily torment. Recognizing this more
clearly as the 'years matured the silent strife',[1]
refusing the comfort of forgetfulness, he had to
extricate himself from the Locke tradition, not
because it was 'false', but because for himself, at
some hours, it was too painfully true. It was the
intellectual equivalent of his uncreative moods, and
of the temper of an uncreative century.

Taken as psychology—not as metaphysics—there
is little in such an account of mental *activity* with
which a modern psychologist—even though he combines with it a metaphysical materialism, and
supposes that the mind is just certain ways of
operation of the body—will treat now as other
than a commonplace. Data for him are facta; he

[1] See *Phantom and Fact.*

60

knows too much about the dependence of every mental event upon former mental events to regard any of their products as simply given to us. For him the activities of the self (however he interprets the phrase) are results of past activities. This assumption is the governing condition of his science and sets its terms of reference. The self in its past activity has been forming and therein experiencing itself — not only in perceptions but in feelings, desires and the rest, in every sort of experiential mode that we can mention. And this prior experiencing determines how it will experience in the future.

But with this word *determines* we are under the feet of one of Coleridge's favourite hobby-horses. He was a resolute free-will man, and his conception of freedom is involved in several of his most characteristic doctrines. "The medium, by which spirits understand each other, is not the surrounding air; but the *freedom* which they possess in common" (*B. L.*, I, 168). "The inner sense has its direction determined for the greater part only by an act of freedom" (*B. L.*, I, 172). "The self-conscious spirit therefore is a will; and freedom must be assumed as a *ground* of philosophy, and can never be deduced from it" (*B. L.*, I, 185). This is no place in which to go into that controversy, but a suggestion may be offered which may make Coleridge's view more acceptable to determinist eyes, and may make my interpretations not seem to be contradicting Coleridge quite so flagrantly.

Suppose we define *freedom* as 'action according to its own laws', and suppose further that in nature there are steps in the kinds of laws which govern events. Physical, physiological, psychological, animal, human laws of behaviour—with perhaps a number of steps in types of human behaviour—might be examples. The step in each case may be supposed to be one of additional complexity of interrelation between events and to involve no abrogation of 'lower-order' laws. Thus a man would be free (and derivatively responsible) if his acts were determined by laws of appropriate complexity; but not free when he is a slave to habit or subjugated by indigestion. This is the sense, I think, in which we say that an insane person has lost his mental freedom. Laws of lower order, physiological or infantile, have stepped into the place of higher-order laws. Similarly a man falling downstairs is obeying the laws of gravitation, but if he were walking down we would say he was moving of his own will. As the Stoic, Chrysippos, said, a cylinder may be made to roll down a plane, but its manner of rolling is that of a cylinder It follows the laws of its own form. Now Coleridge described *genius* as 'the power of acting creatively under laws of its own origination. We may connect this with the suggestion that the will which is free only comes into being with these laws, and, in brief, is them. "That in the soul of man . . . in consequence of which he was a man and without it would not have been, must necessarily be of the same nature and kind with those laws of the universe which acted upon him and which he alone was capable of beholding." (*Philosophical Lectures*, p. 107. See too pp. 184–5 below and *How to Read a Page*, p. 203.)

Coleridge's idealism did not, of course, debar him any more than other idealists from the use of the everyday assumptions we all use—which seem so hard to reconcile with it. He would have agreed with the rest of us that he criticized Shakespeare's plays, and that Shakespeare himself was entirely without, and independent of his, Coleridge's, imagination. This objection to such an idealism— our assumption of the independent existence of other people—is a common-place of philosophy. Coleridge deals with it very frankly. The 'essential prejudice . . . the fundamental presumption, THAT THERE EXIST THINGS WITHOUT US,' he says, 'originates neither in grounds nor arguments, and yet on the other hand remains proof against all attempts to remove it by grounds or arguments.' It 'lays claim to IMMEDIATE certainty as a position at once indemonstrable and irresistible, and yet' it is inconceivable that anything 'extrinsic and alien to our being should become a modification of our being' as it must, he considers, if it is to be known. "The philosopher therefore compels himself to treat this faith as nothing more than a prejudice, innate indeed and connatural, but still a prejudice."

"The other position . . . namely, I AM, cannot so properly be entitled a prejudice. It is groundless indeed; but then in the very idea it precludes all ground, and separated from the immediate consciousness loses its whole sense and import. It is groundless; but only because it is itself the ground of all other certainty."

Few will doubt that these twin positions are 'indemonstrable and irresistible'. But what we are assuming when we assume them is a more difficult question. Coleridge himself spent the second half of his life exploring the region in which he felt a reconciliation lay.

> "The apparent contradiction that the former position, namely, the existence of things without us, which from its nature cannot be immediately certain, should be received as blindly and as independently of all grounds as the existence of our own being, the transcendental philosopher can solve only by the supposition, that the former is unconsciously involved in the latter; that it is not only coherent but identical, and one and the same thing with, our own immediate self-consciousness."

Something like this has, of course, become an accepted truth in genetic accounts of the growth of our concepts of the Self and of the External World—and not only for Idealist psychologists. The Materialist too has his parallel problem, in the lack of any adequate theory to bridge the gap between physiology and consciousness. And he from his side frequently 'solves' it in an analogous manner by an identification. But whereas Coleridge identifies the existence of things with the existence of the self, he reverses the step, and finds the explanation of the self in the behaviour of certain sorts of things. 'Identical' is evidently a very tricky word here. It is noteworthy that 'A is identical with B' often seems very unlike 'B is identical with A'. If Coleridge can write 'there are things = I am' but not 'I am = there are things', this is evidence of ambiguity either in 'I am', or in 'there are things', or in both. As we shall see later (Chapter VII), just what is to be identified with what is the difficult question.

Most of these formulations of doctrine Coleridge drew from Schelling. "In all probability," Shawcross remarks, "not writing with Schelling's works before him, but transcribing excerpts from his notebooks, inserted perhaps many years before." He may well have taken them as the handiest expressions, available to a hurried man, of views which he looked forward to developing in a more exact manner later. The title of Chapter XII in which they occur is: *Of requests and premonitions concerning the perusal or omission of the chapter that follows*— a chapter that in fact was never written. Coleridge evidently felt quite as much dissatisfaction as any sympathetic reader is likely to feel with these formulations, and we should be misguided if we read them with a rigorous eye as though they were finished paragraphs of that 'third treatise of my *Logosophia*' whose announcement at the end of *Biographia Literaria* was promised but not made.

(See Vol. I, 179.) It is legitimate, I think,[1] to take them (knowing their derivation) as merely a preparatory exercise intended by Coleridge to discount certain current assumptions (they are still current in literary circles) about the modes of operation of the mind—assumptions which make the discussion of Imagination as idle as if Coleridge's Esquimau were a party to it. For, although technical psychology has improved almost out of recognition since Coleridge's day, current literary education (as the columns of the best contemporary reviews too much show) has not as yet benefited.

I have reproduced these transcendental idealist formulations because, in spite of their borrowed style, they show Coleridge's prepossessions as a psychologist very clearly. As metaphysics they are, perhaps, inevitably incorrigible. It is not hard to see that *knowledge*, for example, is shifting its senses in several directions in this discussion. Coleridge would perhaps have done better to keep closer to Kant. But as psychology, and it was *as psychology* that the *critic* in the Coleridge of 1801 was most concerned with them, these views of the mind as an activity are a new charter of liberties. From this vantage ground Coleridge was

---

[1] Coleridge's own final opinion supports me. " The metaphysical disquisition at the end of the first volume of *Biographia Literaria* is unformed and immature; it contains fragments of the truth but it is not fully thought out. It is wonderful to myself to think how infinitely more profound my views now are and yet how much clearer they are withal. The circle is completing; the idea is coming round to, and to be, the reality."—*Table Talk*, June 28, 1834; one month before his death.

able to survey a territory for profitable analysis which has not yet been entered upon.

There can be little doubt, in the light of subsequent developments, that Coleridge as against Associationism of the Hartley-Condillac type was right all along the line. But, and here he exemplified a frequent pattern of philosophic advance, what has proved him right has been constructive developments on the part of the very materialistic-mechanistic doctrines that he was attacking—developments of a kind that he did not foresee, made in the teeth of the arguments and exhortations the Coleridge of 1817 was most attached to. Were Coleridge alive now, he would, I hope, be applauding and improving doctrines of the type he, as a metaphysician, thought least promising in his own day. For, when he kept to psychology, he often showed a very curious prescience of the developments to come.

I will close this chapter with a few examples of this foresight which also point directly to the theory of Imagination which is the subject of the next.

Until long after Coleridge, until nearly the end of the nineteenth century, it was officially taught that 'trains of ideas' (associations) were governed by the two great principles of Contiguity and Similarity, important enough laws in their way, but perhaps hardly so precise or so recondite as we should expect the fundamental laws of a science to be. [By Similarity the sight or thought of a monkey may make me think of other monkeys, seen at Benares, say. By Contiguity I may think not of another monkey but of the Ganges.] Some said by way of improvement, noticing both the duplication and the war between similarities and contiguities, that they were governed by Continuity of Interest.

Coleridge was saying this sort of thing:

> Association depends in a much greater degree on the recurrence of resembling states of feeling than on trains of ideas.

> Ideas no more recall one another than the leaves in a tree fluttering in the breeze propagate their motion one to another.

> Again, what is a thought? What are its circumscriptions, what the interspaces between it and another? When does it begin? Where end?—Far more readily could one apply these questions to an ocean billow, or the drops of water which we may imagine as the component integers of the ocean. As by a billow we mean no more than a particular movement of the sea, so neither by a thought can we mean more than the mind thinking in some direction.

> How opposite to nature and the fact to talk of the 'one moment' of Hume, of our whole being an aggregate of successive single sensations! Who ever felt a single sensation? . . . And what is a moment? Succession with interspace? Absurdity! It is evidently only the *licht-punct* in the indivisible undivided duration.

> One travels along with the lines of a mountain. Years ago I wanted to make Wordsworth sensible of this.—(1804, Lipps' doctrine of empathy came in the eighties.)

Coleridge on the self before he read Schelling:

> By deep feeling we make our *ideas dim*, and this is what we mean by our life, ourselves. I think of the

68

wall—it is before me a distinct image. Here I necessarily think of the *idea* and the thinking *I* as two distinct
and opposite things. Now let me think of myself, of
the thinking being. The idea becomes dim, whatever
it be—so dim that I know not what it is; but the
feeling is deep and steady, and this I call *I*—identifying
the percipient and the perceived.—(1801.)

These are utterances—and the collection could
be greatly extended—that make Coleridge seem
to anticipate much that is most fruitful in recent
psychology. In contrast to theories of association
by which a state of mind is represented as a cluster
or composition of revived impressions fished up
from a mental storehouse and arranged around a
sensation given to a passive mind—the whole offered
like a deck of cards to a self or will standing over
against it and able at best to approve or veto or
rearrange it—his conception of the mind as an
active, self-forming, self-realizing system is plainly
an immense improvement. As an instrument for
exploring the most intricate and unified modes of
mental activity—those in poetry—its superiority
seems overwhelming.

We have now to reconstruct his view in the form
which seems most serviceable to the critical purposes
he designed it for.

But, since no ancient opposition of intellectual
methods can ever be safely taken as settled to the
exclusive advantage of either side, we may well
linger for a last paragraph with the metaphysical
question. It can easily be assumed that Coleridge's

doctrine of the mind as a self-realizing activity and Locke's (or James Mill's) view of it as a combination of impressions, ideas and movements, are necessarily in conflict with one another. But—as a general principle which will bear more examination than it ordinarily receives—when two doctrines have *different vocabularies*, and different traditions and assumptions behind them, we cannot reasonably satisfy ourselves, or take either party's word for it that they are as opposed as they seem to be. We could only be satisfied if we were able to perform a perfect analysis exhibiting them in common terms. We need, in other words, to discover just what each is doing, and a means of comparing these doings—a common framework in which the rival speculative machineries can be examined. Such an analysis and such a technique of comparison are beyond our present powers. But until we have them we should be chary of deciding that there is any irreconcilable clash between their results.

In yet other words, the moment we succeed in acting upon our perception that all people who write or talk about these matters are using *language*, and ask, 'How far is language, as employed at present in such matters, to be trusted?' we shall see reasons to wait before concluding that of two such views expressed in conflicting words one must be wrong if the other is right. As we shall see in the next chapter, something rather like a refreshed atomism—a counting of inter-relations—appears again as we develop and apply Coleridge's doctrine. Words are but marks, and in the Neo-Mohist paradox, "Marks reach—the reaching never reaches." The history of philosophy shows clearly enough that fruit comes most often from the cross-fertilization of enemy strains.

CHAPTER IV

No officious slave
Art thou of that false secondary power
By which we multiply distinctions, then
Deem that our puny boundaries are things
That we perceive, and not that we have made.
The Prelude.

COLERIDGE's best-known formulation of the difference between Imagination and Fancy comes at the
end of the first volume of *Biographia* in those
astonishing paragraphs, quoted in the last chapter,
in which he contents himself for the present with
stating the main result of a chapter that was never
to be written. And although many readers have
gathered from them that the distinction is in some
way 'metaphysical'; that the Primary Imagination
is a finite repetition of creation; that the Secondary
Imagination is an echo of the primary; that it
dissolves to recreate or, at least, 'to idealize and to
unify'; and that it is vital, as opposed to Fancy
which 'has no other counters to play with but
fixities and definites' and is 'a mode of memory
emancipated from the order of space and time';
neither Coleridge's grounds for the distinction nor
his applications of it have as yet entered our general
intellectual tradition. When they do, the order of
our universes will have been changed.

Here is a representative application:

> One of the most noticeable and fruitful facts in psychology is the modification of the same feeling by difference of form. The Heaven lifts up my soul, the sight of the ocean seems to widen it. We feel the same force at work, but the difference, whether in mind or body that we should feel in actual travelling, horizontally or in direct ascent, *that* we feel in FANCY.
>
> For what are our feelings of this kind but a motion IMAGINED, with the feelings that would accompany that motion, less distinguished, more blended, more rapid, more confused, and, thereby, co-adunated? Just as white is the very emblem of one in being the confusion of all (1804, *Anima Poetæ*, 101.—My capitals).

This note is perhaps more a test of an understanding of Coleridge's theory than an exposition of it. Yet, when the theory has become a clearly defined speculative instrument, it would be hard to find a better example of its use. Before examining the example, however (see p. 110), the theory must be given as explicit a formulation as I can contrive.

Coleridge begins in *Biographia* (I, 62), after the opposition: "Milton had a highly *imaginative*, Cowley a very *fanciful* mind," [1] by comparing the

---

[1] Mr Eliot's comments on this (*The Use of Poetry*, pp. 29, 58) as begging some question, seem to me to be vitiated by a confusion as to which the question under discussion was. Coleridge here was not advancing any argument; but *giving an example* to show *that the words had been desynonymized.* He would have qualified Mr Eliot's alternative, " Spenser had a highly imaginative, Donne a very fanciful mind." For Spenser and Donne are, in opposite ways, mixed cases. " The great and prevailing character of Spenser's mind is fancy. . . . He has an imaginative fancy, but he has not imagination, in kind or degree, as Shakespere and Milton have."—

relation between fancy and imagination to that between delirium and mania. The ground of the comparison is made clear elsewhere:

> You may conceive the difference in kind between the Fancy and the Imagination in this way, that if the check of the senses and the reason were withdrawn, the first would become delirium, and the last mania (*Table Talk*, June 23, 1834).

But that these results of the removal of the check do not imply an approximation of imagination to mania, appears in this:

> Great wits are sure to madness near allied, says Dryden, and true so far as this, that genius of the highest kind implies an unusual intensity[1] of the modifying power, which detached from the discriminative power, might conjure a platted straw into a royal diadem; but it would be at least as true, that great genius is most alien from madness—yea, divided from it by an impassable mountain—namely, the activity of thought and vivacity of the accumulative memory, which are no less essential constituents of 'great wit' (*Table Talk*, May 1, 1833).

Literary Remains, I, 90. As we shall see, wholes themselves composed of Fancy may have some of the powers of Imagination. " Did Coleridge acclaim Donne? " Mr Eliot asks on p. 72. The right answer is, Yes, repeatedly and especially for his passion: see for example, *B. L.*, II, 56, 65. " To read Dryden, Pope, etc., you need only count syllables; but to read Donne you must measure *Time*, and discover the Time of each word by the sense of Passion." (*Notes on English Divines.*) Donne most often builds, in the mode of Fancy, with imaginative units formed in 'meanings press and screw.'

[1] This may seem to support Pater's phrase 'intensity of perception' (see p. 39), but Coleridge here is not defining Imagination. He is comparing different cases of it in respect of the degree of the modifying power implied by them. He would not have allowed that the modifying power acted in Fancy.

Under these checks of the senses and reason, of the activity of thought and the vivacity of the accumulative memory, the mind in its normal state uses *both* Fancy and Imagination. Coleridge often insisted—and would have insisted still more often had he been a better judge of his readers' capacity for misunderstanding—that Fancy and Imagination are not exclusive of or inimical to one another. He says of Wordsworth's account of them:

> I am disposed to conjecture, that he has mistaken the co-presence of fancy and imagination for the operation of the latter singly. A man may work with two very different tools at the same moment; each has its share in the work, but the work effected by each is very different (*B. L.*, ch. xii, 194).

And again:

> Imagination must have fancy, in fact the higher intellectual powers can only act through a corresponding energy of the lower (*Table Talk*, April 20, 1833).

And he could have reversed the *dictum,* for the counters, the 'fixities and definites' that fancy plays with, are only counters at all, only exist to be played with, through earlier acts of perception. They have come into being, been formed, by earlier acts of Imagination; but, so far as *Fancy only* is now at work, they are not being *re*formed, they are not being integrated, co-adunated into a new perception.

We are on the verge here of a very difficult

75

inquiry into the senses of the words, *unity, integration,* and *one*; or into the problem of the types of unity that mental processes may have. And we can avoid this vast philosophic quagmire only by remembering that here too 'our puny boundaries' are not things that we perceive but that we make. In drawing, with Coleridge, a line between Imagination as a bringing into one—an esemplastic power—and Fancy as an assembling, aggregating power, we must bear in mind the purpose for which we draw it. The importance and the persistence of the purpose, and the utility of the distinction, establish the line, and it has no other establishment. If we were to say, for example, that the division was laid down in Nature, that would be here no more than a grandiose way of referring to the same or other purposes and utilities.

The problem to attack then is not the abstract one: What is unity in itself? (which, apart from concrete examples, is a pseudo-question) nor: What ought we to mean by 'unity'? (interesting though this might be on another occasion) but: What hypothesis can we invent which will be useful to us in describing and reflecting upon a difference we notice between certain examples which, we shall agree, are different.

Let us begin with the examples which Coleridge treats in most detail—the two opposed passages from *Venus and Adonis.* (See Raysor, *Coleridge's Shakespearian Criticism,* I, pp. 211–218; or *Literary Remains,* II, 53–60.)

76

As Fancy we have:

> Full gently now she takes him by the hand,
> A lily prison'd in a gaol of snow,
> Or ivory in an alabaster band;
> So white a friend engirts so white a foe.
> > *Venus and Adonis*, 361–364.

Of Fancy, Coleridge says:

(1) That it is 'the faculty of bringing together images dissimilar in the main by some one point or more of likeness distinguished' (Raysor, I, 212).

(2) That these images are 'fixities and definites' (*B. L.*, I, 202), they remain when put together the same as when apart.

(3) That the images 'have no connexion natural or moral, but are yoked together by the poet by means of some accidental coincidence' (*Table Talk*, June 23, 1834).

(4) The activity putting them together is that of choice, which is 'an empirical phenomenon of the will'—that is, *not* the will as a principle of the mind's being, striving to realize itself in knowing itself, *but* an exercise of selection from among objects already supplied by association, a selection made for purposes which are not then and therein being shaped but have been already fixed.

Fancy, indeed, is the mind's activity in so far as Hartley's associationism seems to apply to it.

Now let us examine the lines in detail and test

these descriptions upon them. The two middle lines are those which show Fancy most clearly.

Adonis' hand: Venus' hand: : lily: gaol of snow

Adonis' hand and a lily are both fair; both white; both, perhaps, pure (but this comparison is more complex, since the lily is an *emblem* of the purity which, in turn, by a second metaphor is lent to the hand). But there the links stop. These additions to the hand *via* the lily in no way change the hand (or, incidentally, the lily). They in no way work upon our perception of Adonis or his hand. It would be difficult for them to do so in view of other things in the poem:

With this she seizeth on his sweating palm (line 25)

and the only whiteness he has shown so far is that of anger,

Twixt crimson shame, and anger ashy pale. (verse 13.)

The same absence of interaction between the parts of the comparison is shown equally with *prison'd* and *gaol of snow*. In contrast to the implied efforts or will to escape of the *prison'd* hand, a lily would be the most patient of captives.[1] And anything *less* resembling a gaol of snow that Venus' hand could hardly be chosen—except in *two* uncombined 'points of likeness distinguished', two accidental coincidences, namely that the gaol and the hand are both enclosures and both white.

[1] Compare,

> Emprison her soft hand, and let her rave.

But Venus' hand is not a static enclosure, and the whitenesses will seem less compatible the more we consider them.   In another kind of poetry, we might take the incompatibility of our feelings about flesh and snow as a positive part of the interaction. A Goddess' hand might well be inhuman; but not here. So, too, with one further link that might be suggested. Snow melts; and Venus has said, above,

> My smooth moist hand, were it with thy hand felt,
> Would in thy palm dissolve, or seem to melt.
>
> (verse 24.)

But here, observably, there is no interaction; there is no such mutual interchange of properties. It would be as absurd here to think Venus cold because she is being compared to snow.

It is clear—and becomes clearer on closer inspection—that, unless we give the lines a strained reading which the context does not invite, there is no relevant interaction, no interinanimation, between these units of meaning.

I have taken them here (following Coleridge) as *images*; that is, as units that might be seen 'in the mind's eye', or otherwise *imaged*; but the same would be true whatever the distinguishable units we introduced were, whether these were notions, feelings, desires or attitudes. However, we take them we shall find that *the links* between them are accidental, contribute nothing to the action; though *the absence* of relevant links does. Pondering the links does not enrich the poem. The additional possible connections ¹—they come easily whenever we linger attentively over any comparison—are here irrelevant and merely distracting. And the cross-connections between the links (between whiteness and purity, for example) with all their possibilities in other kinds of poetry, are equally beside the purpose here.

Another way of describing this would be to say that Shakespeare is not here realizing—or attempting to realize—the contact of the hands in words: either as felt by Adonis, or by Venus, or as seen by himself or by us as possible witnesses. He is doing something quite different. If we say that he is *describing* their hands in these lines we should recognize what

¹ Mr A. P. Rossiter permits me to insert an interesting note in which he explores a further connection: " I think some interaction can be made out between Lily: snow: : ivory: alabaster. There is, for example, a colour-contrast: lilies and ivory have a tannish tinge which is not normally seen in snow or alabaster; and Venus may be taken to be whiter than Adonis. (I am not relying on a mental picture!) If the terms are changed, I think this is clear.

> Full softly now his hand is in her power
> Like alabaster held in ivory
> Or snow imprisoned in a lily-flower
> White friend enclosing whiter enemy. . . .

But you have to have hunted round both versions a lot before you think, ' But ivory isn't as white as snow.' And, in practice (unless this were an example of something you expected to be abstruse) you never would; the initial yield isn't enough to make you go on, as it is with the ' bright star.' There is a sort of AA-sign, NO THROUGH ROAD at the corner of these examples of Fancy. You can go down, but you have to get out and ramble. And that is what all this excogitation is—the melting snow, the ' virgin ' lily, etc., etc. With the meteor passage, the interanimation is not only between ideas moved by words, but between contexts; the whole falling-star situation is relevant to (and modified by) the Venus situation, and *vice-versa*. But no context made up of snow, lilies, ivory and alabaster bands is relevant to or modified by the hand situation."

different activities can be put behind this word. I glance later (Chapter IX) at some of the historical and other questions suggested by the existence of quite different types of describings. They are obviously not to be arranged simply as good and bad. And here Shakespeare is not making a bad description of a kind in which any modern novelist could beat him; he is doing something else. He is making pleasing collocations that are *almost* wholly unconnected with what he is writing about.

Why he is doing this (and what this is) are large questions. The answer would be partly historical; it would show that the purposes that poets may pursue are much more various than we ordinarily suppose. It would be partly psychological; it would show that the structure or *constitution* of poetic meanings may vary from extreme federalism, as here, to the strictest centrality—from a case, as here, where the meanings of the separate words are almost completely autonomous (and their grouping is for a purpose which does not concern them) to the case, to be illustrated in a moment, where the several units of meaning surrender almost all their local independence in a common co-operative purpose.

If we like to say here, with Coleridge, that knowing the perilous nature of his subject in *Venus and Adonis*—how easily cloying—Shakespeare is deliberately practising 'alienation and aloofness' in his own and his readers' feelings, 'dissipating the reader's notice', the speculation can at least serve to indicate the effect. The commonest characteristic effect of Fancy is the coolness and disengagement with which we are invited to attend to what is taking place. As Coleridge remarks, here Shakespeare 'works exactly as if of another planet, as describing the movements of two butterflies' (Raysor, I, 218).

> This beauteous combat, wilful and unwilling
> Show'd like two silver doves that sit a-billing.

The last line of the four that Coleridge quotes is slightly different. We may see in it the working of Imagination as opposed to Fancy.

> So white a friend engirts so white a foe.

Venus is Adonis' friend in two senses. She is his lover, and, if he had yielded to her, she would have been his preserver. With the second sense, there comes a reach and a repercussion to the meaning, a live connexion between the two senses and between them and other parts of the poem, consiliences and reverberations between the feelings thus aroused, which were missing in the other lines. How different this is from Fancy we can see by the experiment of considering that snow may also be a lily's preserver—a picked lily packed in snow and, obviously, is its foe. Neither fact enters relevantly in Fancy.

We can turn now to Coleridge's instance of Imagination: Adonis' flight.

> Look! how a bright star shooteth from the sky
> So glides he in the night from Venus' eye.

How many images and feelings are here brought together without effort and without discord—the beauty of Adonis—the rapidity of his flight—the yearning yet helplessness of the enamoured gazer—and a shadowy ideal character thrown over the whole (Raysor, I, 213).

Here, in contrast to the other case, the more the image is followed up, the more links of relevance between the units are discovered. As Adonis to Venus, so these lines to the reader seem to linger in the eye like the after-images that make the trail of the meteor. Here Shakespeare is realizing, and making the reader realize—not by any intensity of effort, but by the fulness and self-completing growth of the response—Adonis' flight as it was to Venus, and the sense of loss, of increased darkness, that invades her. The separable meanings of each word, *Look!* (our surprise at the meteor, her's at his flight), *star* (a light-giver, an influence, a remote and uncontrollable thing) *shooteth* (the sudden, irremediable, portentous fall or death of what had been a guide, a destiny), *the sky* (the source of light and now of ruin), *glides* (not rapidity only, but fatal ease too), *in the night* (the darkness of the scene and of Venus' world now)—all these separable meanings are here brought into one. And as they come together, as the reader's mind finds cross-connexion after cross-connexion between them, he seems, in becoming more aware of them, to be discovering not only Shakespeare's meaning, but something which he, the reader, is himself making. His understanding of Shakespeare is sanctioned by his own activity in it. As Coleridge says: "You feel him to be a poet, inasmuch as for a time he has made you one—an active creative being."

This, then, is an *observable* difference from which we set out, though it is unhappily not true that all can observe it equally or equally clearly. But that is a general difficulty afflicting all studies of mental processes since the conditions of the observations vary with the skill and prepossessions of the reader. The account we please to give of the difference, our preference for one account of it rather than another, is another matter. Whether we observe the difference, and how, depends upon our habits in reading. Whether—having observed it—we choose to *describe* it in one way or another, depends upon the ideas and the methods we find most convenient *in general* in discussing our mental affairs; which, in turn, depend upon the purposes of the discussion.

Anyone who is well acquainted with Coleridge's ways of discussing Fancy and Imagination will notice that I have, at several places above, translated them in terms which might sometimes have been repugnant, as suggesting mechanical treatment, to Coleridge himself. In place of 'the power by which one image or feeling is made to modify many others and by a sort of *fusion to force many into one*,' I have used phrases which suggest that it is the number of connexions between the many, and the relations between these connexions, that give the unity—in brief, that the co-adunation is the inter-relationship of the parts. If we are careful to separate the *description* of a process or experience from the experience itself, this should not mislead. The terms in which we describe the experience will vary with the purposes we need the description for. Admitting this, we shall not suppose that units corresponding to these terms actually occur in the experience. We do not suppose that the grain in a photograph corresponds to a grain in the field we photograph. Similarly here, what we find, by inspection, in the experience, depends upon the terms—the assumptions, conceptions, expectations . . . with which we inspect it. These are intro-duced by the technique of inspection. If we were naïve enough to suppose that an inspection (and resulting description) of an experience could be perfect—introduce nothing, omit nothing, and in no way distort—this artificiality of descriptions might distress us. But a perfect description, if such a description introduced or omitted nothing, would just be the experience itself over again. We should be left by it where we were, and be not a jot ad-vanced towards our purpose in making a description, which is to gain a systematic method of comparison between experiences.

Our descriptions must apply. Whatever the machinery of distinctions they employ and thereby impose upon the experiences, they must record differences in the experiences which they do not impose, which are prior to and independent of the imposed distinctions. It is the merit of Coleridge's Fancy and Imagination as descriptive devices that they note such actual differences in the experiences they apply to. With this, a first step towards systematic comparisons between the structures of the meanings of poetry has been made. And, still more important, with it the way towards a further technique of comparison has been opened. But to explore it successfully we must assume that our descriptions are products of our technique, not simple copies of the experiences we are describing; and that we may change them within limits *without* thereby changing our view of the point of difference between the experiences we are comparing with their aid.

Under this charter of technological liberty let me attempt another description of the difference between Fancy and Imagination—a re-formulation which may be of assistance in the next chapter, where I consider Coleridge's remark that 'the sense of musical delight, with the power of producng it, is a gift of the imagination', and his doctrines of the relation of metre to poetry.

In Imagination the parts of the meaning—both as regards the ways in which they are apprehended and the modes of combination of their effects in the mind—mutually modify one another.

In Fancy, the parts of the meaning are apprehended as though independent of their fellow-members (as they would be if they belonged to

86

quite other wholes) and although, of course, the parts together have a joint effect which is not what it would be if the assemblage were different, the effects of the parts remain for an interval separate and collide or combine *later*, in so far as they do so at all.

The points which most pressingly need elucidation in these formulations, concern:

(1) The parts of a meaning; in what sense, here, have meanings parts?

(2) Apprehension; how, if at all, is the apprehension of a meaning to be separated from its effects?

(3) Mutual modification; what is this?

(4) How are we to separate such joint effects as all collocations must have—merely through the normal relativity (or inherent unity) of mental process—from the special modes of combination of effects on which the distinction, largely, turns?

In attempting to answer these questions, we are face to face with the chief difficulty of all such work, and can escape it only by holding firmly to this guiding principle: that we are not trying, in our descriptions, to say *what happens*, but framing a speculative apparatus to assist us in observing a difference.

(1) Meanings may be said to have any parts which, for our purposes, we find useful as instru-

ments in comparing them. Here some of the most useful parts seem to be:

Awareness of the words as *words*: as sensory presentations (shapes on the paper, movements of the organs of speech, sounds associated with them), with whatever else, and there may be much, that must be included in an account of what words, as opposed to their meanings, are.

Sense: i.e. thoughts of things, of states of affairs, that arise with perception of the words; their plain prose meaning, as we sometimes say; together with such imagery as may, in certain types of minds, accompany these thoughts and be a medium or support to them.

Feeling: i.e. reverberations or emotional or practical attitudes towards the things, or states of affairs, thought of in the sense.

Tone: i.e. attitudes of the reader to the writer (or of writer to reader) implicitly assumed or explicitly controlled at every point in all writing.

Under each of these headings will appear (as we use higher and higher powers of the speculative analytic instrument) myriads of distinguishable 'units', whose connexions with one another, and with 'units' under other headings are an inexhaustible field for enquiry.

(2) The apprehension of the meaning of a set of words is, for a *reader*, a selection from their effects upon him. (For a *writer*, this *may* be reversed, the finding of the words be an effect of an apprehension.) I take *apprehension*, in the formulations

88

above, arbitrarily: as the more immediate part of our response to the words. It is separated, on the hither side, from our mere recognition of the words as *these* not *those* words; and, on the farther side, from later ramifications and reverberations of effects due to our simultaneous and successive apprehensions—this first-order 'superficial' response to them. But apprehension is not to be equated simply with Sense as above described. Feeling and tone factors come into the first stages of the interpretation of words in poetry. We may have taken up an attitude to the what-not, that is being talked about, and an attitude to the poet, *before* any definite thoughts of the what-not have developed. The thought often grows under their control; and may in some instances and for some purposes be regarded as a specialization of Feeling. But the peculiar reference of thoughts to the things-they-are-of gives them modes of interaction with one another which are lacking in the case of feelings. And this interplay is studied as their logical compatibility or incompatibility, and other relations. The patterns of our thoughts *represent*, in various ways, the world we live in. The patterns of our feelings represent only a few special forms of our commerce with it.

(3) With parts of a total meaning so conceived, their 'mutual modification' becomes a way of describing the development of the response which is this meaning. After apprehending how *a bright star shooteth from the sky* we respond to Adonis' gliding otherwise. And reciprocally the develop-

ment of Feeling (and Tone) from *bright star shooteth* is modified by our knowledge, for example, that Adonis is going to his death. Latent possibilities in it are called out. In comparison, latent possibilities in *lilies* and *gaols* of *snow* are not called out by the co-presence in the response of Adonis' and Venus' hands. Our apprehension of them stays at the sketchy stage it reached with our first bare understanding of the words.

(4) Yet, of course, the line

A lily prison'd in a gaol of snow

as a comparison for their hands, does have a joint effect. There is a resultant unity of meaning—the unity which any utterance has no matter what the internal relations of its parts. It has a meaning, that is to say. If I write

cockatoo glass plum bat . . .

and we take this to be an utterance—if we put the parts together to form any whole—in this whole, whatever it is, effects from the parts (however we take them) come together into some joint effect. So with all utterances. What we have to consider are differences in the mode of formation of a joint effect.

The example (any such example) is puzzling—which, here, is instructive—in a number of respects. Being without syntax, we are free to combine the parts as we please. As separate apprehensions of meanings for the separate words, they are not set in any fixed relations to one another to begin with. And this mere freedom gives these parts an opportunity, *if we avail ourselves of it*, to modify one another from the start which would be lost if we gave the words a definite syntax and formed a sentence.

This mutual modification, did it occur—most readings will exercise only Fancy—would be Imagination, a lowly and elementary example of it; and of no literary importance because, being contextless, the mutual modification is at the mercy of the freaks of the reader's interpretation, and thus any valuable result would be the reader's private poem. The fact, however, that an absence of syntax is a favourable condition for Imagination is important. It explains why languages whose syntax we do not understand sometimes seem inherently poetical: *e.g.* literal, word for word translations from 'primitive' tongues or from Chinese; why ambiguous syntax is so frequent in Shakespeare; and why, in much of the modern verse which derives from Mr Ezra Pound, it is easy to mistake a mere freedom to interpret as we will for controlling unity of sane purpose—that is, purpose integrated with and relevant to our lives as wholes.

The danger of such a remark as this, however, is that it may lead us to conceive Imagination in terms of value, to say that it is mutual modification *to a good end*. This was undoubtedly most often Coleridge's view. But Imagination, as I have described it, can be shown in trivial examples. And

Fancy can be shown in important matters, though the range of powers, from good to bad, of Imagination seems, as we should expect, to be greater than that of Fancy. In Imagination, as I have taken it, the joint effect (worthless or not) ensues only through and after a reciprocal stressing, one by another, of the parts as they develop together, so that, in the ideal case, all the possible characters of any part are elicited and a place found for them, consentaneous with the rest, in the whole response. In Fancy, on the other hand, only a limited and fixed selection of the possible characters (and thus possible effects) of the parts are admitted into the process. The stressing is done by the final effect, which ruthlessly excludes all but a limited number of interactions between the parts, setting strict frontiers of relevance about them. Doubtless the ideal case of Imagination is rare; if enough of the possibilities of the part-meanings come in we overlook any that must stay out. With Fancy, we either 'overlook' them in quite another sense, we voluntarily and expressly ignore them; or we let an awareness of their *irrelevance* in to gain a mixed effect, of burlesque for instance:

> And like a Lobster boyl'd the Morn
> From black to red began to turn.

But this is a special complex use of Fancy, not to be mistaken for the norm. In simple Fancy we just ignore what is discrepant, as when we see pictures in the fire or shapes in the clouds. It is no part of such visions that they are seen in fire or cloud. We, like Polonius, succeed in seeing what we want to best when we forget the coals or the cumulus. But when, in Imagination, Antony compares the change in himself to the changes of the clouds, the halves of the similitudes are equally active:

> Sometime we see a cloud that's dragonish;
> A vapour sometime like a bear or lion,
> A tower'd citadel, a pendant rock,
> A forked mountain, or blue promontory
> With trees upon it, that nod unto the world
> And mock our eyes with air: thou hast seen these
>   signs;
> They are black vesper's pageants.

Eros.   Ay, my lord.
Ant.   That which is now a horse, even with a thought
        The rack dislimns, and makes it indistinct,
        As water is in water.
Eros.   It does, my lord.
Ant.   My good knave, Eros, now thy captain is
        Even such a body: here I am Antony;
        Yet cannot hold this visible shape, my knave.

Or when, for Prospero,

>   The great globe itself,
> Yea, all which it inherit, shall dissolve
> And, like this insubstantial pageant faded,
> Leave not a rack behind.

there is no mere collocation of some aspects of one thing (carefully excluding others) with some aspects of another. We are invited to stretch our minds, and no one can flatter himself that he has ever

93

finished the process of understanding such things. In neither passage is there a phrase which does not carry, at first unnoticed, secondary and tertiary co-implications among their possibilities of interpretation. These supernumerary meanings need not be explicitly reflectable in articulated thought. They may be so, as with *black vesper's pageants*; but the bridging echoes may pass only between feelings. We may not be able then to make any analysis, but the felt recession, roominess and richness of the meaning, in great instances, are not to be mistaken. The two I have cited are both 'philosophical', and it may be thought that *this* and not the imaginative process is the explanation. But the same living multiplicity is observable in

> And there is nothing left remarkable
> Beneath the visiting moon

or in,

> Here are sands, ignoble things,
> Dropt from the ruin'd sides of kings.

But these are Fancy:

> Trade, which like Blood should circularly flow,
> Stopp'd in their Channels, found its Freedom lost:
> Thither the Wealth of all the World did go,
> And seem'd but Shipwrack'd on so base a Coast.
> *Annus Mirabilis*, 2.

> To see this Fleet upon the Ocean move,
> Angels drew wide the Curtains of the Skies;
> And Heav'n, as if there wanted Lights above,
> For Tapers made two glaring Comets rise.
> *Annus Mirabilis*, 16.

94

The expatiation on the possible nature of these Comets in the next two verses makes their status in Fancy very plain. Consider the effect of asking (illegitimately here, but relevantly if this were Imagination) why Heaven should need more Tapers by which to watch this naval battle? Or what Curtains (clouds?) would, without the care of the Angels, have hidden it from Heaven?

> The Foe approach'd, and one, for his bold Sin,
> Was sunk (as he that touch'd the Ark was slain :)
> The wild Waves master'd him and suck'd him in,
> And smiling *Eddies* dimpled on the Main.
>
> *Annus Mirabilis*, 94.

To attempt to read this in the mode of Imagination would be to experiment in mania. It is a product of Fancy and is offered to Fancy only. It may be well here to recall one of Coleridge's most liberating remarks: "Do not let us introduce an Act of Uniformity against poets."

For convenience I have taken, as examples of Fancy and Imagination, short passages of a few lines only. But the contrast might be illustrated equally with whole works. Thus, in prose fiction, the detective novel is a type of Fancy, but any presentation of an integral view of life will take the structure of Imagination. The units imaginatively disposed may themselves be products of fancy; and, conversely, a series of imaginative passages may be arranged (as beads on a string) in the mode of Fancy—a structure characteristic of Hardy.

Some points in these explanations of Imagination and Fancy will, I hope, be made clearer in the next chapter. I will close this with some remarks on the use of these words as implying different values. *Imagination*, as Coleridge uses it, is, of course, very often a term implying higher values than *Fancy* (critics who point this out with an air of discovery or complaint should re-read him). The conception was devised as a means of describing the wider and deeper powers of some poetry. It is a descriptive psychological term in the sense that it points to facts which explain certain values. Subject to the conditions noted in the passage about mania quoted on p. 74, the exercise of the Imagination is, for Coleridge, more valuable than the operations of Fancy. We can, if we wish, relax these conditions, and make the terms purely descriptive. We shall then have instances of Imagination which are valuable and instances which are not, and we must then go on to contrive a further theory, a theory of values which will explain (so far as we are able to do so at present) these differences of values. [This is the procedure I attempted to follow in *Principles of Literary Criticism*.] Coleridge does not so separate his psychology from his theory of value. His theory of Imagination is a combination of the two, and there is much to be said in favour of this more difficult order of procedure. It does more justice to the unity of mental process, and, if such an exposition is understood, there is less risk of suggesting that the value aspects of our activities are independent of, or supernumerary to, their nature—less risk of our taking the same question twice as though it were two questions, not one.

Coleridge's treatment pins itself to a factual difference between some events in our mind and others. It is a difference which cannot be adequately described by taking account only of the events in isolation. We must take account of their place and function in the whole activity of the mind —and of this not only as an individual life but as a representative of what he calls the '*all in each* of human nature' (*B. L.*, II, 64). A description which must reach so far becomes, I think, inevitably valuative. But in saying this I am taking sides in an old and still far from concluded debate—the question, simplified,. being: whether a *complete* factual account of a life would leave anything to be discussed, under a separate irreducible head, as its value? It may well be, though, that this description of the question (and perhaps any description) is ambiguous. Our descriptions are verbal machines exposed to the danger that we ourselves misuse them after we have made them. The facts they try to render would soon be lost to us if we had to rely upon these descriptions.

Fortunately we have a more direct and surer method of identifying the work of the Imagination: namely, through the Imagination itself. In spite of all aberrations there is a persistent tradition—as constant as any theory of human nature and its conditions would allow us to expect—which recognizes acts of Imagination. Literally they are *recognized*: the *all in each* finds again in them the same enlargement. Arnold said that great poetry interests the permanent passions; but this, as so often happens, splits what is one into two. For the passions are *in* the poetry and the poetry is only the way this interest and these passions go in it. No description of imagination is of any use to those who do not otherwise sometimes know this way—as poets; or know when they are in it, as readers; yet it is the way—however often fashion, miscomprehension, obstructive pre-possessions, or dullness may hide it from us.

"On the IMMEDIATE," quotes Coleridge from Schelling, "which dwells in every man, and on the original intuition, or absolute affirmation of it (which is likewise in every man, but does not in every man rise into consciousness) all the *certainty* of our knowledge depends; and this becomes intelligible to no man by the ministry of mere words from without. The medium, by which spirits understand each other, is not the surrounding air; but the *freedom* which they possess in common, as the common ætherial element of their being, the tremulous reciprocations of which propagate themselves even to the inmost of the soul." Without this: "No wonder, that, in the fearful desert of his consciousness, he wearies himself with empty words, to which no friendly echo answers, either from his own heart, or the heart of a fellow being;

or bewilders himself in the pursuit of *notional* phantoms, the mere refractions from unseen and distant truths through the distorting medium of his own unenlivened and stagnant understanding! To remain unintelligible to such a mind, exclaims Schelling on a like occasion, is honour and a good name before God and man."

CHAPTER V

THE SENSE OF MUSICAL DELIGHT

I am fully aware that what I am writing and have written will expose me to the censure of some as bewildering myself and readers with metaphysics; to the ridicule of others as a schoolboy declaimer on old and outworn truisms or exploded fancies; and to the objection of most as obscure.—*The Friend.*

"A POEM contains the same elements as a prose composition," said Coleridge in beginning his discussion of metre, "the difference therefore must consist in a different combination of them, in consequence of a different object being proposed" (*B. L.*, II, 8). He goes on to discuss different possible objects, or purposes, and does not here linger to consider what these 'elements' may be; but we must linger, for upon our view of these elements our understanding of his theory of metre will depend.

We may take the *elements* of a composition to be just the words—the separable words or phrases into which a grammatical analysis would reduce it. But if we take them so, we soon meet various troubles. Some of the words will have several distinct meanings; characteristically a word in a poem will have supernumerary active meanings which are cut out in prose. Again the meanings of words in poetry combine otherwise than in prose. In brief the *use* of words in poetry is frequently different from their use in prose. If we identify a word merely by its spelling and its grammatical functions, we must say that the same words in poetry and prose may have quite different meanings. But it is their meanings we are throughout concerned with, so the remark that poetry and prose both contain the same elements (*i.e.* English words) would take us very little distance.

The point may be brought out equally well by recalling that a word, as this is defined for grammatical and lexicographical convenience, is an abstraction from an utterance. We print it separately on the paper, giving it an artificial independence which it does not possess in the utterance. But criticism and analysis of poetry (or prose) is concerned only with utterances. There is thus a perpetual and insidious risk in analysis that we shall misconceive the structure of the utterance through taking the separate grammatical units as the units of meaning. The point deserves italics. *Words are not necessarily the units of meaning.* And a word by itself apart from an utterance has no meaning—or rather it has too many possible meanings. Only as its possible meanings combine with those of other words does it gain any meaning we can take an interest in. What is said here of a word, applies evidently in a less degree to larger units, the sentence for example.

These and similar reflections make one thing clear: that the literary conception of *words* as the elements either of poetic or prose compositions is inadequate for serious studies. It would be easy to collect a bookful of examples from would-be serious students, in which lack of reflection as to what we are talking about when we talk of words has deprived their remarks of utility. One instance here will be enough to represent the kind of comment I have in mind. "In Poetry," says Mr Herbert Read in his *English Prose Style*, pp. x–xi, "the words are born or re-born in the act of thinking. . . . Does it follow that Poetry is solely an affair of words? Yes: an affair of words adequate to the thought involved. An affair of one word, like Shakespeare's 'incarnadine', or of two or three words, like 'shady sadness', 'incense-breathing Morn', 'a peak in Darien', 'soft Lydian airs', 'Mount Abora', 'star-inwrought', or of all the words necessary for a thought like the *Divine Comedy*." He continues, "Paradoxical as it may seem, we now see that Poetry may inhere in a single word, in a single syllable, and may therefore be without rhythm; Prose, however, does not exist except in the phrase, and the phrase always has rhythm of some kind." That all this is but self-mystification appears plainly as soon as we notice that *Shakespeare's* 'incarnadine' is the word in its context as Shakespeare uses it. Print it in a lipstick advertisement and note what becomes of its poetry! Only while we supply its context does it retain its poetic effect, and the same is true, with slight differences in degree, due to additional context, of the other examples.

The first step towards remedying these stultifying

confusions—which afflict almost all discussion of rhythm and metre—is to reflect carefully upon what we may mean by *a word*. We have a scale of possible meanings; to sort them out and arrange them is more important that it may seem, since this scale gives us the paradigm for a large class of words the fluctuations of which share the same pattern. Among them will be found *Poem, Rhythm* and *Thought*, to mention three only. A mastery of the paradigm also allows us to translate into one another some differing accounts of Fancy and Imagination.

A full treatment of the fluctuations of the word *word* would fill a volume. That we permit our meanings, at such a cardinal point, to remain in such an unnecessary tangle is an instructive fact, a ground for believing that the development of science has hitherto been somewhat one-sided. I shall make no attempt here to cover the range of these fluctuations, and omit or note only in the sketchiest fashion the distinctions which are less directly relevant to our purposes.

1. By *a word* we may mean an individual occurrence with a date and place amongst occurrences— a single act of speech, a set of movements of the organs of speech with the emission of a sound, or the making of a set of marks on paper; or the hearing, on a single occasion, of that sound, or the sight of the marks. Or if overt speech is not occurring, we may have in its place the mental substitute for such a single act of speech.

2. But by *a word* we commonly mean something more recondite than this. We are thinking with a fiction that represents many such acts of speech; and a word becomes something that a million people use on the same day, and that successive generations go on using through hundreds of years. If we ask how this fiction is constructed, we at once have half the abstruser problems of semasiology on our hands. I wish to avoid them here, and it will be enough, perhaps, to notice only that *words*, in this sense, are abstractive fictions whose function is to collect, for comparison, classes of 'their' use. By the aid of these fictions we describe innumerable words (Sense 1, speech-acts) as examples of 'the same word' (in Sense 2). Apart from speech-acts there are obviously no words. The detail of the ways in which we thus create objects, though sometimes very relevant to criticism, is less important for us here than the recognition that this fictional mode of classification equally supplies all the other objects, units or entities (poems, rhythms, meanings, thoughts, emotions) with which literary criticism concerns itself. Inadequacies in this quasi-automatic abstractive machinery (and there is reason to suspect that there are many) supply us with unreal problems and prevent clear investigation of the facts. It is thus a prime part of the business of criticism to re-examine all these, its assumed instruments, and the method by which we have been given them.

The collection, for dictionary purposes, of speech-acts as examples of 'one word' combines two principles. One principle takes note of similarities and changes in the form of the speech-acts; the other watches their functions, or meanings. The combination has forced a certain artificiality upon our choice of the aspects or parts of the meanings which are taken into the account. Thus we commonly take a part only of the meaning of a speech-act as being *the word's meaning*, and count the rest of its meaning as our response to this meaning. Just where this line is to be drawn is, of course, for our arbitrament; but, forgetting this, we easily make it a matter for desperate conjecture. This artificiality is the occasion, however, for extremely important differences in our practice both in reading and in analysing the meanings of words— variations so important that much of the history of literature must some day be written in terms of them (cf. Chapter IX). These changes in part explain the very different problems which critics in different ages have thought most important, and, further, the different ways in which they have formulated those problems which are perennial. Two extreme cases among these varying attitudes are easy to describe. In between, are steps harder to define, as we draw our line to include more or less of our total response as the word's meaning. But these steps are recognized in good reading and divide poetry into kinds.

3. By *a word* we may mean merely such and such a sort of marks on paper, or heard sound, or movement of the speech-organs, any example of which

is the stimulus to (or, in the speaker's case, the accompaniment or outcome of) the response we call an understanding of it. That is to say we *can* take, as the word, merely the sign. But we rarely do this. In the process of recognizing the signs we invest them with qualities which, *as signs*, they do not possess. As in merely reading marks on paper we invest them with their sound and movement, so further we invest their sound and movement with further qualities which also come to them from our past experience with similar speech-acts. Rapidity, weight, force, as well as other characters less easily named, characters much concerned in the tone and feeling the words can convey, are among them. These immediate sensory accruments to the signs are often very plastic and changeable, but sometimes they are obstinate enough to explain why the finest meanings cannot make the words which convey them sound right [1]—a point which needs emphasizing perhaps, since so often what we call the 'resonance', 'tang', or 'quality' in the sound of words is but a reflection from their meaning.

4. So far I have not included any meaning in *the words* either as bare signs or as invested signs. But as we swing over from an attitude to words as signs to an attitude to them as *containing in themselves* a part or whole of the meaning we give to

[1] Flaubert will be a good witness here: Comme si la plénitude de l'âme ne débordait pas quelquefois par les métaphores les plus vides, puisque personne, jamais, ne peut donner l'exacte mesure de ses besoins, ni de ses conceptions, ni de ses douleurs, et que la parole humaine est comme un chaudron fêlé où nous battons des mélodies à faire danser les ours, quand on voudrait attendrir les étoiles.

them, we get quite another sense for *word*. We shall find it difficult perhaps, in the middle of this paragraph of analysis, to take up this attitude. To say that a word is or contains in itself its meaning will seem only a short (and sometimes convenient) way of saying that it is a sign with a certain meaning appropriated to it. But, if we are not explicitly asking ourselves questions about how we read, but just discussing literary matters, we do, on innumerable occasions, not only *talk* but actually think as though the words and their meanings are one and the same. We put its meaning into our working definition of a *word*. ("Few men, I will be bold to say," said Coleridge, "put more meaning into their words than I.")

Anyone who doubts this may consider the parallel case of *poem*. How often, when we discuss a poem, do we *not* include a meaning as well as the marks on the paper, in our acting definition? A meaning is always what we are talking about, never the signs. What we say about the poem is true (if it is) only about the meaning. It is inapplicable, in fact nonsense, as commentary on the signs. And this is not a matter of ellipsis, of our laziness and disinclination to make elaborate analytic statements. This investment of the words with a meaning is an essential part of the right reading of them—as essential, to choose an obvious parallel, as seeing the marks on a canvas as a picture-space is sometimes in the right viewing of a picture. The parallel may be pressed: there are pictures with which we should be more aware of the canvas than with others. So too there are poems with which we should be more aware of the words, as separate from their meaning, or as possessing only a limited 'dictionary' meaning, than with others. Pope at his best, as opposed to Keats at his best, will serve as examples.

This shift in our attitude to words—from one extreme case where they are taken as conventional signs to the other extreme case where they are read as living inexhaustible meanings—has many steps. As a rule a part of the meaning is put into the word and the rest is left to be our response to this meaning. The division is not hard to mark, perhaps, in

> Through wood and dale the sacred river ran,
> Then reached the caverns measureless to man,
> And sank in tumult to a lifeless ocean:

or in

> Dim, as the borrow'd beams of Moon and Stars
> To *lonely, weary, wandering* Travellers,
> Is *Reason* to the *Soul*.

But in

> Thou still unravished bride of quietness
> Thou foster child of silence and slow time

or in

> She looks like sleep—
> As she would catch another Antony
> In her strong toil of grace

it is another matter. In the first two it is not hard to give such meanings to the words as will explain their further effect, and justify the rest of the meaning. In the last two, no meanings short of the whole meaning we can find in them seem adequate to account for what they do.

This scale—between words taken as bare signs and words into which some part or the whole of their meaning is projected—is a paradigm for the fluctuations of many literary descriptive terms. I have cited *Poem, Rhythm* and *Thought*: the last of these may need a slight explanation. At one extreme we have the Behaviourist view of thought as sub-vocal talking; at the other (cf. my quotation from Herbert Read, p. 102) thought is everything that can take place in the mind; in between, thought may be opposed, as a part of the mental activity, to perception, emotion, feeling, wishes or action. Usually we have to guess from what else we know of an author in what sense to take it. Another example is *Plot*, which, to the distress of commentators on *The Poetics*, ranges from mere Fable or Argument—such an account of the events in a play as might be put on a post-card—to Action, in a sense in which it turns out on examination to be nothing short of the whole play itself, including all the thoughts and all the characters, and all the response of a qualified spectator.

As the critical terms are slid along this scale, the characteristic critical doctrines emerge into plausibility. Thus, were the paradigm more exactly studied, we would be able to avoid much fruitless refutation of views which have never been put forward. We should have, moreover, the beginning of a technique of translation or mediation between doctrines framed in different senses of their terms. Imagination and Fancy provide an example of this. Coleridge, we have seen, tends at times to state their difference in terms of a fusion, a co-adunation, of the objects contemplated in the poem —the objects in Fancy remaining separate, but in Imagination merging into one another. I have translated him into an account which, for convenience of analysis, dispenses with this projection and discusses them as differing types of interaction between parts of a total meaning for the passage. But I am not in so doing denying the validity of his projective account.

The projection of its meaning into a word is an instance of Imagination, parallel to those instances of empathy given by Coleridge in the passage cited at the beginning of Chapter IV. As we project a motion into a form so we project meaning into words. But such projection is not enough to make a passage imaginative in the further sense with which the critic is concerned. The meanings thus projected must interact with one another in the modes described in the preceding chapter. It seems likely, however, that most poetry which is markedly imaginative will naturally be read as though its meanings were inherent in the words; and that some of the poetry of Fancy, on the other hand, will be best read otherwise—with a clear and recognized distinction between the words and the meanings we take from them. But how far this speculation could be substantiated is a matter for detailed investigation.

Whatever further inquiry may show as to the extent to which these shifting attitudes to words influence the structure of poetry, there can be no doubt about their relevance to the formulation of critical theories. This becomes especially clear with theories of the functions of metre. If by *the words* we understand the sensory signs, we shall raise a number of questions about metrical form, and about its relations to the meaning of the poetry, which will not arise at all if by *the words* we understand the signs as already invested with their meanings. A large part of the work that has been done on prosody has no direct relevance to poetry read on the latter assumption.[1] Its application is to verse written and read with an attitude to words that sets them over against their meanings—as with the bulk of eighteenth-century poetry for example.

Coleridge, in his discussion of the functions of metre, wavers between the two conceptions; sometimes taking metre as a sensory pattern of the signs, sometimes making it the very motion of the meaning. And this is part of the explanation of the oddly disjointed condition of his argument.

After noting the superficial mnemonic unity that verse confers, and 'the particular pleasure found in anticipating the recurrence of sounds and quantities'

[1] For a justification of this remark and for some allied considerations see *Practical Criticism*, Appendix A, 4.

(*B. L.*, II, 9)—two important subsidiary points—
he unluckily introduces a definition of a poem in
terms of *purpose, truth* and *pleasure.*

> A poem is that species of composition, which is
> opposed to works of science, by proposing for its
> *immediate* object pleasure, not truth; and from all other
> species (having *this* object in common with it) it is
> discriminated by proposing to itself such delight from
> the *whole*, as is compatible with a distinct gratification
> from each component part.

Coleridge was fond of this definition, introducing
it on several occasions in his Lectures. He evidently
considered it one of the best things he had done.
But the more patiently we examine it, the less satisfactory shall we find it. Not only is there ambiguity
in its chief term *pleasure* (as well as in the opposed
term, *truth*) but the final phrase 'a distinct gratifica-
tion from each component part' seems to be
incorrigibly misleading in spite of its obscurity.

First as to *pleasure*. Coleridge was evidently aware
when he lectured in 1811 that *pleasure* was an
inadequate word here.

> The immediate object of science was the communica-
> tion and acquirement of truth, the immediate object
> of poetry is the communication of pleasure. Yet it
> would be acknowledged by all that when they read
> Newton's *Principia* or Locke's works the immediate
> object was not pleasure, but to obtain truth which might
> hereafter enlighten the pursuit of pleasure, or some-
> thing nobler, for which we have not a name, but distinct
> altogether from what in the ordinary language of com-
> mon sense can be brought under the name of pleasure,

but which was expressed in the sacred writings as a peace that passeth all understanding, the delight of which could never be known but by experience, which, consisting of no difference of parts, but being in itself entire, must be altogether unknown, or fully known (Raysor, II, 75).

Is it capricious to bring this into connection with what he is going on to say (*B. L.*, II, 12) of the poet as bringing 'the whole soul of man into activity'? It may be so, but certainly this view of pleasure links it with 'that sort of pleasurable emotion; which the exertion of all our faculties gives in a certain degree; but which can only be felt in perfection under the full play of those powers of mind which are spontaneous rather than voluntary, and in which the effort required bears no proportion to the activity enjoyed.' Coleridge's pleasure is a pleasure of activity, no passive satisfaction, that is clear; but, if so, his choice of the phrase '*immediate* object' is the more unfortunate. For such pleasure cannot be immediately aimed at. The tenor of his description is still to confuse pleasure as the ultimate effect (the something nobler) with pleasure as the immediate lure of interest.

Coleridge failed to notice that in this description of pleasure (he may have kept no note of it: we have only a report by a Mr Tomalin) he had something with which to go beyond an opposition of *pleasure* to *truth*, either as an immediate or as an ultimate end. "In other works the communication of pleasure may be the immediate purpose; and though truth, either moral or intellectual, ought to be the *ultimate* end, yet this will distinguish the character of the author, not the class to which the work belongs" (*B. L.*, II, 9). But Coleridge is throughout using, if not the 'character of the author', at least the mode of operation of the author's mind as his principle of division. He could very easily have brought moral truth (as 'the subordination of the faculties of the whole soul of man to each other, according to their relative worth and dignity' (*B. L.*, II, 12)) into adjustment with this description of pleasure and thus avoided the worst troubles of his definition.

How awkward these were can be seen in an amusing example on the page that follows:

> But if this should be admitted as a satisfactory character of a poem, we have still to seek for a definition of poetry.

This, I am afraid, is only a wild attempt to escape unfortunate consequences, for the definition of poetry must ensue from that of a poem as directly as that of circularity does from that of a circle.

> The writings of PLATO and Bishop TAYLOR and the "Theoria Sacra" of BURNET, furnish undeniable proofs that poetry of the highest kind may exist without metre, and even without the contra-distinguishing objects of a poem. The first chapter of Isaiah (indeed a very large portion of the whole book) is poetry in the most emphatic sense; yet it would not be less irrational than strange to assert, that pleasure, and not truth, was the immediate object of the prophet.

This could only show that Coleridge had chosen those 'contra-distinguishing objects of a poem' wrongly. It is characteristic of S. T. C. that he should thus point out the objections to his formula and yet try to evade them. The evasion, however, is much less characteristic than the honesty. He could, of course, have said, more successfully, that these things were poetry in another—even in the most emphatic—sense; or, dropping the *immediate*, have said that Isaiah combined both truth and pleasure. What he did was to introduce one of the finest red-herrings in all the literature of criticism.

> In short, whatever *specific* import we attach to the word, poetry, there will be found involved in it, as a necessary consequence, that a poem of any length neither can be, or ought to be, all poetry.

But the question was not about any other parts of Isaiah but about his poetry.

These are Coleridge's wrigglings with his 'pleasure-truth' opposition. It is not to be saved without a reinterpretation of both terms which he did not here seriously attempt. But we have still to consider the last clause of his definition. Coleridge hoped by adding it to distinguish poetry from prose romances, which for him also had pleasure as their *immediate object*. He rephrased it several times: in the 1811 lectures it reads, 'admitting pleasure from the whole, consistent with a consciousness of pleasurable excitement from the component parts' (Raysor, II, 78). His numerous glosses and explanations show, I think, some lack of confidence about it.

The trouble is that he is trying to do several different things with it at once. When he says, for example, that whatever is put into metre 'must be such as to justify the perpetual and distinct attention to each part, which an exact correspondent recurrence of accent and sound are calculated to excite' (*B. L.*, II, 10) a glance at the foot of the page where he remarks that 'Philosophic critics of all ages' deny 'the praises of a just poem . . . to an unsustained composition, from which the reader collects rapidly the general result, unattracted by the component parts' shows us one thing he is doing with it. He is saying that a poem is something to be really read, not skimmed like a newspaper. But so must any close-knit writing be.

Coleridge hoped to do something much more ambitious with it—to deduce a necessary connection between metre and poetry. But he would have to show that in no other way than by metre could we be forced to attend to all the parts in order to enjoy a whole. The examples of a detective novel (in ideal perfection), or of a cross word puzzle, defeat him. His formulation, 'a perpetual and *distinct* attention to each part' (here *part*, I think, evidently means foot) also invites a serious misunderstanding of the normal process in reading verse. Surely, unless we are deliberately *scanning* poetry as we read, looking for 'an exact correspondent recurrence of accent and sound', we rarely give a 'perpetual and distinct attention to each part'. I may quote Coleridge against Coleridge here: "As far as metre acts in and for itself, it tends to increase the vivacity and susceptibility both of the general feelings and of the attention. This effect it produces by the continued excitement of surprise, and by the quick reciprocations of curiosity still gratified and still re-excited, *which are too slight indeed* to be at any *one moment objects of distinct consciousness*, yet become considerable in their aggregate influence. As a medicated atmosphere, or as wine during animated conversation; they act powerfully, *though themselves unnoticed*" (*B. L.*, II, 51).

Attention—even perpetual and distinct—was not, of course, for Coleridge the same thing as explicit and conscious noting. 'Distinct', of course, is the dangerous word. Coleridge tried again with the phrase 'continuous and equal attention', which is somewhat safer. A better account would go into more detail and insist that in the reading of poetry we give a fuller and more entire response to the words than in any other reading; that we include not only an intellectual apprehension of their meanings, but an experimental submission to them, the fullest realization of their varied powers upon us as these are reflected in their sound and movement.

But Coleridge is really saying this in another form when, in explanation of his definition, he appeals to 'that pleasurable emotion, that peculiar state and degree of excitement that arises in the poet himself in the act of composition' (Raysor, II, 77).

The very assumption that we are reading the work of a poet supposes that he is in a continuous state of excitement; and thereby arises a language in prose unnatural, but in poetry natural. As every passion has its proper pulse, so will it likewise have its characteristic modes of expression (Raysor, II, 68).

And what is the 'something else' which turns animated passionate prose into poetry?

> In order to understand this we must combine a more than ordinary sympathy with the objects, emotions, or incidents contemplated by the poet, consequent on a more than ordinary sensibility, with more than ordinary activity of the mind in respect of the fancy and the imagination (Raysor, I, 164).

And we must add to this, from that crowning description at the close of Chapter XIV of *Biographia*, 'a more than usual state of emotion with more than usual order; judgment ever awake and steady self-possession, with enthusiasm and feeling profound or vehement' (*B. L.*, II, 12).

Indeed it seems only fair to Coleridge to conclude that when he writes (*B. L.*, II, 49), "It might be easily explained likewise . . . how this balance of antagonists became organized into *metre*," he is not doing what people who say that something is easily explained, but do not explain it, are most often doing—that is dodging by the chief difficulty. Coleridge could, and in a scattered way did, explain it.

Why he did not say somewhere outright that the organization of language into metre was a part or aspect of the self-organization of the mind that is uttering itself in poetic composition is puzzling,

especially if we recall his letter to Godwin in 1800,
"Are not words etc. parts and germinations of the
plant? And what is the law of their growth? In
something of this sort I would endeavour to destroy
the old antithesis of words and things, elevating, as
it were, words into things and living things too."
And he was to say, "The rules of the Imagination
are themselves the very powers of growth and
production", and again, "It is a fellow-growth from
the same life even as the bark is to the tree. No
work of genius dares to want its appropriate form."

The bond, in other words, between metre and
poetry—which remains unintelligible so long as we
separate words from their meanings and treat them
as mere signs fitted into a sensory pattern—becomes
an evident necessity if we consider the words as
invested with their meanings. With words so invested, their metrical movement is no longer so
distant a thing as a *counterpart* to their meaning.
The relations of the form to the meaning—whether
dactylic measures suit gay or spondaic grave subjects, and so on—cease to be a matter for profitable
inquiry. The movement of the verse becomes the
movement of the meaning; and prosody, as a study
of verse-form apart from meaning, is seen to be a
product of unwary abstraction. In saying that
'the sense of musical delight, with the power of
producing it, is a gift of the imagination,' Coleridge
set aside the conventional conception to restore a
wholeness to our view of the act of speech—a
wholeness we are in endless danger of overlooking,

for reasons that a study of the ambiguity of the word *word* makes plain. The perceived relations between temporal parts of an utterance, which seem to the ear to constitute good metre, derive from relations between parts of its meaning. The *simulacra* [1] that may be composed with nonsense verses should not deceive us here; the pleasure that they may give is of another order and comes from other sources; it can, as Coleridge pointed out, be given by the jejunest compositions.

But if 'the sense of musical delight is a gift of the imagination', how is it that it can be given by poems, *Venus and Adonis*, for example, or *Hero and Leander*, or pre-eminently, *The Fairy Queen*, which are chiefly works of Fancy? One answer is that, though a poem may be Fancy as regards the mode of interaction, one with another, of its separable parts, the consistency of its *total meaning*, when it is such that 'the sense of musical delight' arises, is imaginative. The structure may be built of bricks, and brick be bound to brick with mortar—to use the image that accords with Fancy—and yet the whole structure have a unity of another order altogether, an architectural, which is here an imaginative, unity. And it may be this other unity which produces 'the sense of musical delight'. It is thus that Spenser 'has an imaginative fancy'. Conversely a structure whose parts are held together one to one, not as bricks by mortar but as the cells

[1] See *Practical Criticism*, pp. 229–233, for a further discussion of these points.

of a living organism grow together— to use the image which accords with Imagination—may *as a whole* have no imaginative unity. Such are the ravings of mania. Verses which, knot by knot, are highly imaginative *may* lack all power of producing the sense of musical delight.

But the difficulty still remains that single lines, or passages too short for a larger grace to arise, may possess the power in spite of being all Fancy in the discernable linking of their meanings. It may be met, in part, by recalling (see p. 110) that the projection of meaning into words is itself an imaginative process. As the sound and movement of the line seem to become a body for the meaning, much is happening that offers opportunity for order and disorder. We know at present very little about this process, and suppose it, in our simplicity, to be simple. But here, at the other end of the scale, in a microscopic field, the same alternatives of confusion or coadunation present themselves.

Thus behind what has too often been taken to be 'a mere superadded merit of fine sound' we have to recognize, as the source of our delight in poetry, a principle of sane growth in the mind. And this is the subject of the next chapter.

CHAPTER VI

GOOD SENSE

" Believe me, my dear James! it is no musty old saw but a maxim of life, a medicinal herb from the garden of experience, that He alone is *free* and entitled to the name of gentleman, who knows himself and walks in the light of his own consciousness. But for this reason nothing can be rightly taken in, as a part of a liberal education that is not a means of acquainting the learner with the nature and laws of his own mind—as far as it is representative of the human mind generally. . . . All knowledge, I say, that enlightens and liberalizes, is a form and a means of self-knowledge, whether it be grammar, or geometry, logical or classical. For such knowledge must be founded *on principles*, and those principles can be found only in the laws of the mind itself. . . . For (as I have long ago observed to you) it is the fundamental mistake of grammarians and writers on the philosophy of grammar and language, to suppose that words and their syntax are the immediate representatives of *things*, or that they correspond to *things*. Words correspond to thoughts, and the legitimate order and connection of words, to the *laws* of thinking and to the acts and affections of the thinker's mind. . . . Read this over till you understand it. God bless you."—*Letter to James Gillman* (*ætat* 19), 1827.

No one who reads *Biographia* carefully will fail to notice that though his conception of Imagination is the main instrument Coleridge uses, yet when he is applying it to examples, or deciding whether a passage is an instance of it or not, he has another— apparently quite different—principle to appeal to; namely, Good Sense.

'Good sense' stands first in Coleridge's list of characteristics requisite for the highest excellences in a dramatist, and this just after one of his most awe-inspiring descriptions of Imagination (Raysor, I, 207).

It is by 'good sense, and a moderate insight into the constitution of the human mind' that we are to conclude that such things as Cowley's

Begin, begin thy noble choice,
And let the hills around reflect the image of thy voice,

are "rhetorical caprices . . . the native product neither of the fancy nor of the imagination; that their operation consists in the excitement of surprise by the juxtaposition and *apparent* reconciliation of widely different or incompatible things. As when, for instance, the hills are made to reflect the image of a *voice*. Surely, no unusual taste is requisite to see clearly, that this compulsory juxtaposition is not produced by the presentation of impressive or delightful forms to the inward vision, nor by any sympathy with the modifying powers with which the genius of the poet (here Pindar is being translated) had united and inspirited all the objects of his thought" (*B. L.*, II, 67–8).

I confess that I find Coleridge a little unfair here. The two lines quoted seem to me clearly an example of Fancy, though a lowly one. Coleridge takes the description of an echo as the reflection of the image of a voice to be a daring '*apparent* reconciliation of widely different or incompatible things'. But surely it is hardly more than a generalization, easily to be brought within the scope of 'the faculty of bringing together images dissimilar in the main by some one point or other of likeness distinguished'. But as to the idleness of the lines in the context there seems no ground to dispute his opinion.   I have quoted the passage to show the nature of his appeal to Good Sense and as a forewarning of its dangers.

It is by its difference from 'the language of GOOD SENSE' also that he condemns Gray's Sonnet—

> In vain for me the smiling mornings shine

"The second line,

> And reddening Phœbus lifts his golden fire;

has indeed almost as many faults as words.   But then it is a bad line, not because the language is distinct from that of prose; but because it conveys incongruous images, because it confounds the cause and the effect, the real *thing* with the personified *representative* of the thing; in short, because it differs from the language of GOOD SENSE" (*B. L.*, II, 58).

It is both instructive and amusing to notice how easily this description of faults could be turned into an account of imaginative excellence:

We have only to write for 'it conveys incongruous images'—'it reconciles opposite and discordant qualities'; for 'it confounds cause with effect, the real *thing* with the personified *representative* of the thing'—'it blends the idea with the image, lends to the image an intellectual life transferred from the poet's own spirit' and these accounts may seem only to reflect a determination to find fault and a resolution to admire.   If we were to argue the matter from the two standpoints, would it be possible, by applying the doctrine of imagination, to *demonstrate* that either view was right? We can easily invent for the admirer subtle considerations based on distinctions between types of metaphor—those where the image stands clearly apart from what it images, with an inter-in-animation between them; and those where the two are so close together that the metaphor produces something in which neither is distinguishable—claiming for Gray that Phœbus and his fire are here one thing that is first *reddening* and then *golden*; or that Phœbus' red is growing more apparent and so *reddening*, but that of course it is known that the *real* colour of his fire is *golden*. Equally easily, we could produce still more subtle reasons for Coleridge, to show that such influence as *reddening* (the effect) exerts upon Phœbus necessarily negates and cancels *lifts* (the cause) since the sun is not setting but rising; and that the logical imbroglio produced by this (whether Phœbus does or does not combine well with *his fire*) obfuscates the whole emotional response, creating here a bewilderment contrary to the heartening intention prescribed by the context. To which again the admirer might reply: 'What heartening context? Phœbus rises *in vain* for him and he *is* bewildered'. The argument [1] as it may be conducted is familiar enough. But the points here to consider are whether the doctrine of Imagination can supply conclusive

---

[1] I personally would incline to a middle view in the matter and think the line not notably either good or bad; the line in the sonnet that strikes me as really extraordinary being

To warm their little loves the birds complain

which sticks out strangely from the rest.

arguments in such cases, and where Good Sense comes in.

We must not be misled by the close of Chapter XIV:

"Finally, GOOD SENSE is the BODY of poetic genius, FANCY its DRAPERY, MOTION its LIFE, and IMAGINATION the SOUL that is everywhere, and in each; and forms all into a graceful and intelligent whole." This is a peroration in an eighteenth-century manner, not designed to be taken too seriously. Coleridge comes nearest to stating the place of Good Sense in criticism in a later passage, where he is discussing Wordsworth's view that poetic diction is 'arbitrary, and subject to infinite caprices, upon which no calculation whatever can be made'. We are to consider what sort of calculation any critical distinctions enable us to make.

"If it be asked, by what principles the poet is to regulate his own style? . . . I reply: by principles, the ignorance or neglect of which would convict him of being no *poet*, but a silly or presumptuous usurper of the name! By the principles of grammar, logic, psychology! In one word by such a knowledge of the facts, material and spiritual, that most appertain to his art, as, if it has been governed and applied by *good-sense*, and rendered instinctive by habit, becomes the representative and reward of our past conscious reasonings, insights, and conclusions and acquires the name of TASTE."

This is not 'in one word', it is in fifty. But it brings out very clearly the relation, for Coleridge, between two senses of *principle*—as conscious reflective thought and as controlling tendency. "I regard that alone as genuine *knowledge* which, sooner or later, will reappear as power" (Snyder, *op. cit.*, 72). But the appeal here to grammar, logic and psychology is evidently dangerous. And we can so easily misconceive their place in poetic and critical practice; similar misconceptions so much affect all the ways of our life; such risks everywhere attend the reaction of incomplete theory upon judgment, that Coleridge's point here may be sharpened a little. Not all power is a blessing to us, and not all knowledge that reappears as power is, in another sense, genuine. It may derive from mere theoretical manipulation, unsupported by experience, and then is sometimes called 'cleverness'.

The question is: Do we yet know enough about what we are doing when we try to analyse a passage of poetry to settle its merits or demerits *by argument*? The 'yet' is there to suggest that our present theoretical knowledge is only a beginning. In view of the immense improvement in our powers that we owe here to Coleridge, it would be idle to set bounds *now* to what may be possible. The question then is *not*: Can man ever hope to know enough to settle such things in some cases? (To this a proper reply, I suggest, would be: We may hope so!) It is: Can the knowledge that is at present available about the mind settle such matters? And to this the answer must be a firm No.

Discussion in terms of our present knowledge has its use in helping us to see what assumptions are likely to be surreptitiously guiding our opinions, and how insufficient and misleading they may be; but *there* its practical service ends. What should guide our decisions is something larger, more delicate and more reliable than our opinions about how the mind works, either in general or in particular instances. What should guide us is our experience of life and literature—not as represented hazardously and schematically in formulatable opinion, but as it is available in a power of choice, 'the representative and reward', as Coleridge calls it, 'of our past conscious reasonings, insights and conclusions'. It will be the modes and capacities of distinguishing that have been developed in these past reflections, rather than the *conclusions* we came to, that become the source and sanction of the choice.

And we must add to Coleridge's account our past *un*conscious learning from the results in us of past choices. For comparatively little of the influence of past experience upon present discrimination goes through the special process of being explicitly recognized in conscious theory, a process which may be supposed in these matters as often to befog as to clarify. And here is the danger of identifying Good Sense (the developed power of choice or, in other words, sanity; cf. 'the vivacity of the accumulative memory', p. 47) with 'the principles of grammar, logic and psychology'.

For men to whom these principles were perfectly known (in the sense of being fully and satisfactorily excogitated) and never for a moment forgotten, the identification might do no harm. But they are as yet so imperfectly known, and what little is known about them is as small a part of what would need to be known if they were to guide us, that we need to be extremely careful in using them. None the less it is still more dangerous not to use them (with discretion) since conscious reflection is our best and quickest method (however many its disasters may be) of correcting unconscious mal-practice. We need 'knowledge how'; and, after a certain stage of reflection has been passed, explicit 'knowledge of' our 'how' is not its enemy.

The use of such distinctions as that between Fancy and Imagination in criticism may be stated compendiously by comparing them to speculative instruments. In a passage immediately following my last quotation, Coleridge expressly compares a critical theory to a microscope. How are we to distinguish one kind of language from another? Is it not "By meditation, rather than by observation? And by the latter in consequence only of the former? As eyes for which the former has predetermined their field of vision, and to which, as to *its* organ, it communicates a microscopic power?" (*B. L.*, II, 64). The difficulty is, of course, that though a microscope may show us much that we could not see without it, we still need a technique to recognize what we see with it and to make sure that we are looking at what we think we are looking at, what we need to look at, and nothing else. And this technique is what Coleridge means by Good Sense.

Good Sense has sometimes a rather sinister sound as a critical watch-word. It is a banner under which every kind of stupidity and every kind of prejudice willingly fight. Even Coleridge, who is so often an exemplar of Good Sense in criticism, is not incapable, in his lesser hours, of using its colours to advance and excuse objections based on careless, inattentive, unresponsive and un-resourceful reading. If I now examine in some detail what I take to be the worst instance, this will be chiefly because this evil is so frequent in other writers and partly to make what has been said about his merits seem less prejudiced.

The instance is Coleridge's dealings with Words-worth under the fifth heading of Wordsworth's characteristic defects: "Thoughts and images too great for the subject . . . a disproportion of thought to the circumstances and occasion" (*B. L.*, II, 109).

I am concerned here with his third example; but the first shows that Coleridge was already beginning to nod.

It is a well-known fact, that bright colours in motion both make and leave the strongest impression on the eye. Nothing is more likely, too, than that a vivid image or visual spectrum, thus originated, may become the link of association in recalling the feelings and images that had accompanied the original impression. But if we describe this in such lines as:

> 'They flash upon the inward eye,
> Which is the bliss of solitude!'

in what words shall we describe the joy of retrospection, when the images and virtuous actions of a whole well-spent life, pass before that conscience which is indeed the *inward* eye: which is indeed '*the bliss of solitude*'?

With what words indeed! And to whom shall *that* vision appear? Coleridge has forgotten that some eight years before, in connection with his finest analysis of imagination, in the lectures of 1808 (Raysor, I, 216), he had expressly described these lines as 'grandly and appropriately said'. He seems here to be exemplifying, as a critic, the very defect with which he charges Wordsworth, and I ought not perhaps to accuse him of using the colours of Good Sense.

But with his comments on *The Ode on the Intimations of Immortality* he is very wantonly misusing argument to exploit his own misconceptions against the poet, and, as such, the process is highly interesting and repays close examination. It gives an admirable exercise in interpreting metaphor.

The last instance of this defect (for I know no other than these already cited) is from the Ode where, speaking of a child, "a six-years' darling of a pigmy size", he thus addresses him:

> "Thou best philosopher, who yet dost keep
> Thy heritage! Thou eye among the blind,
> That, deaf and silent, read'st the eternal deep,
> Haunted for ever by the Eternal Mind,—

Mighty Prophet! Seer blest!
On whom those truths do rest,
Which we are toiling all our lives to find!
Thou, over whom thy immortality
Broods like the day, a master o'er the slave,
A presence that is not to be put by!"

Now here, not to stop at the daring spirit of metaphor which connects the epithets "deaf and silent", with the apostrophized *eye* (1): or (if we are to refer it to the preceding word, philosopher) the faulty and equivocal syntax (2) of the passage; and without examining the propriety of making a "master *brood* o'er a slave" (3), or the *day* brood *at all*; we will merely ask, what does all this mean? In what sense is a child of that age a *philosopher*? In what sense does he *read* "the eternal deep"? In what sense is he (4) declared to be "for ever haunted" by the Supreme Being? or so inspired as to deserve the splendid titles of a *mighty prophet*, a *blessed seer*? (5) By reflection? by knowledge? by conscious intuition? or by *any* form or modification of consciousness? These would be tidings indeed; but such as would presuppose an immediate revelation to the inspired communicator, and require miracles to authenticate his inspiration. Children at this age give us no such information of themselves; and at what time were we dipped in the Lethe, which has produced such utter oblivion of a state so godlike? There are many of us that still possess some remembrances, more or less distinct, respecting themselves at six years old; pity that the worthless straws only should float, while treasures, compared with which all the mines of Golconda and Mexico were but straws, should be absorbed by some unknown gulf into some unknown abyss.

But if this be too wild and exorbitant to be suspected

as having been the poet's meaning; if these mysterious gifts, faculties, and operations, are *not* accompanied with consciousness; who *else* is conscious of them? or how can it be called the child, if it be no part of the child's conscious being? . . . In what sense can the magnificent attributes, above quoted, be appropriated to a *child*, which would not make them equally suitable to a *bee* (6), or a *dog*, or a *field of corn*: or even to a ship, or to the wind and waves that propel it?

I will consider the points I have numbered in order:

(1) Taking the eye to be deaf and silent, we could appeal to 'Blind mouths!' in *Lycidas*; and even though the justification might not be so simple as that which Ruskin found for Milton, it would be not less sufficient. If the eye here is the visionary responsive power as opposed to the discursive analytic power, may we not read 'deaf and silent' as 'not distracted by the need to listen for rumour of that from which no sound comes; or by the effort of speaking upon that of which nothing can be said'?

(2) The syntax is 'faulty' only in that the reader may require to reflect. He may have to notice that *eye* is metaphorical already for *philosopher*—that the two conjointly then have a meaning that neither would have apart. 'An idea in the mind is to a Natural Law as the power of seeing is to light', said Coleridge himself. As an eye, the philosopher is free from the need to do anything but respond to the laws of his being. *Deaf* and *silent* extend the

metaphor by perfectly consentaneous movements—with the silence of light, it describes itself and dwells in *us* only as far as we dwell in *it*' (*The Friend*, Sect. 2, Essay 11). The child will not hear (cannot understand) our words; and he will tell us nothing. That which Wordsworth would derive from him he cannot give; his silence (as we take it through step after step of interpretation, up to the point at which it negates the whole *overt* implication of the rest of Wordsworth's treatment) can become the most important point in the poem. We might look to Lao Tzu to support this: 'Who knows speaks not; who speaks knows not'. But it is enough to quote, from Coleridge himself, "the words with which Plotinus supposes NATURE to answer a similar difficulty. 'Should anyone interrogate her, how she works, if graciously she vouchsafe to listen and speak, she will reply, it behoves thee not to disquiet me with interrogatories, but to understand in silence even as I am silent, and work without words'" (*B. L.*, I, 166).

(3) Masters, *in general*, we agree, do not brood over slaves in any sense of brood. No one will deny the inappropriateness of the image for masters in Rome, South Carolina, the Congo, or Sian fu; but in one instance and that the only relevant instance—the relation of God to his servants in the Christian scheme, the only master-slave relation that Wordsworth is concerned with here—it is perfectly appropriate. And so with *day*. What more natural metaphor for the relation of an im-

mortality to its nursling than that of the day to the young growth of spring which it is drawing up? Moreover that very growth itself, the responsive, eager unfolding is what Wordsworth is pointing to as the child's response. In what way does he *read* 'the eternal deep?' By this very growth.

(4) The child is not, by Wordsworth, said to be haunted by anything: it is the deep that is haunted —not that this makes, I think, very much difference.

(5) Surely, as with *philosopher* so with *Seer* and *Prophet*. They are metaphorical for 'truly responsive to the influences upon them'. (Pursuing that same self-creative, self-realizing growth, which Coleridge has postulated as the highest activity of the mind, through the most active period of growth, the period which gives the adult, as an outcome, most of the relatively static items of his universe.) Surely in this the child may be allowed to be a Seer and a Prophet. Coleridge himself would have to admit him to be a creator.

(6) Finally, why should Wordsworth deny that, in a much less degree, these attributes are equally suitable to a bee, or a dog, or a field of corn? What else had he been saying with his

> And let the young lambs bound,
> As to the tabor's sound!

And what else is Coleridge himself to say in Appendix B of his *Statesman's Manual*? "Never can I look and meditate on the vegetable creation without a feeling similar to that with which we gaze at a beautiful infant . . . as the accidental and dividuous in this quiet and harmonious object is subjected to the life and light of nature . . . which shines in every plant. . . . But what the plant is by an act not its own and unconsciously— that must thou make thyself to become . . . in that light of consciousness which inflameth not, and with that knowledge which puffeth not up!''

What has happened that Coleridge should have been so obtuse here? Why should he be labouring in such a trough of literalism? He is elsewhere to defend Wordsworth from just such misunderstanding. There is no answer to this; for the suggestion that Coleridge was suffering from professional jealousy and resenting the claims of 'the six-years darling' to be the 'best philosopher' is not to be put seriously. I will quote his amends:

> The ode was intended for such readers only as had been accustomed to watch the flux and reflux of their utmost nature, to venture at times into the twilight realms of consciousness, and to feel a deep interest in modes of inmost being, to which they know that the attributes of time and space are inapplicable and alien, but which yet cannot be conveyed save in symbols of time and space. For such readers the sense is sufficiently plain, and they will be as little disposed to charge Mr Wordsworth with believing the Platonic pre-existence in the ordinary interpretation of the words, as I am to believe, that Plato himself ever meant or taught it (B. L., II, 120).

Similarly, we may, if we wish, take all the alleged attributes of Wordsworth's child as fictions, as part of the myth. The poem will not be therefore, to a fit audience, any the weaker. My comments on Coleridge's misunderstandings do not aver that the Ode is a piece of scientific psychology. Nor would I say that—apart from some twenty lines, five or six of which are 'truths that wake, to perish never'—it is at Wordsworth's highest level. But its weakest lines deserve respect as the frame of what they support.

I have discussed these less happy moments in Coleridge's detailed criticism at some length because their occurrence brings up so forcibly the question: What, after all, is the practical utility of literary theory? There are a number of sound enough answers. One is that we shall in any case use theories, and that good theories will protect us from worse. Another is that persons with literary interests to-day frequently suffer from lack of exercise in careful and sometimes arduous thinking. And this the understanding of a good theory entails. A third is that the theory of literary analysis is at an extremely interesting point in its development, on the point of making, through experiment, those contacts with actuality that would transform it into a science, and a science from which very important practical utilities may be expected to result.

But apart from these answers, the assumptions which give rise to doubts as to the value of literary theory deserve attention, for they are connected with the general disparagement of intellectual and theoretical effort, in literature as in life, which has been characteristic of our time. They give us a convenient subsidiary field in which to examine the general revolt against reason, which shows itself most flagrantly in mid-European politics, but is to be noticed, in varying forms, everywhere.

Part of this despair of reason certainly comes from previous misconception and over-estimation of its powers. When a man who has supposed that reason could settle matters for him discovers that it cannot, he not unnaturally looks for some other guide—forgetting that the mind has no guides but itself and that reason is an aspect of the mind. But the terms Reason and Mind change places with one another disconcertingly. Coleridge was accustomed to state this problem of the place of theory in life by a Platonic division (*Republic*, 510) between *Understanding* (that is, theory) and *Reason* (that is, the entire operation of the mind). The Reason is concerned with *Ideas*, a technical term here, for Coleridge defined as follows: "Those truths, namely (supposing such to exist), the knowledge or acknowledgment of which require the whole man, the free will, no less than the intellect, and which are not therefore merely speculative, nor yet practical, but both in one" (Snyder, 100). The Understanding, on the other hand, is 'the rightful sphere of Logic'. The Reason is the source of Principles, the Understanding the faculty of Rules. "The Reason is all *end, summa finium*, the Understanding all means, *summa mediorum*. The rules are in all cases means to some end" (Snyder, 110), and he illustrates this last remark with reference to Neo-Classic misapplications of Aristotelian 'rules' to tragedy.

The decision as to ends rests with Reason, 'the whole man', as much in the approval or disapproval of a passage of poetry as in a political choice; but the Understanding (or Theory) is not merely a manipulating machine. Our theoretical understanding of what we are doing is a partial reflection of the whole activity of the mind—whence both its services and its dangers. We have become used—since psycho-analysis—to conceiving consciousness as a somewhat erratic product of unconscious processes, and are uncomfortably aware that our conscious aims and beliefs may be a distorted reflection of our deeper needs and wishes. But psycho-analysis is also showing us this—that sanity is an order in the whole mind more extensive than, but of the same type as, that order in our consciousness which we study as logic. "All things that surround us, and all things that happen to us," Coleridge thought, "have but one common final cause; namely the increase of consciousness in such wise that whatever part of the *terra incognita* of our nature the increased consciousness discovers, our will may conquer and bring into subjection to itself under the sovereignty of reason" (*The Statesman's Manual*, Appendix B).

But we have to be wary of mistaking elaborated theory for increased consciousness. And yet our theory and our living are not, except in so far (and this is usually some distance), as one or both are in disorder, opposed or discontinuous. The judgment that a passage is good is an act of living. The examination and description of its merits is an act of theory. The act of theory (since theory is incomplete) may always misrepresent it. Equally the act of living may misjudge it. But, though theory may mislead and corrupt judgment, as the history of criticism shows us too painfully, judgment without some theory is blind. Yet in no case can theory take the place of judgment. "Could a rule be given from *without*, poetry would cease to be poetry, and sink into a mechanical art. . . . The *rules* of the IMAGINATION are themselves the very powers of growth and production. The *words*, to which they are reducible present only the outlines and external appearance of the fruit" (*B. L.*, II, 65). What Coleridge says here applies to all our choices, moral, philosophical or political. There is no measuring-rod virtue in any theory. We must use them as we use a microscope—not as we use a centrifuge or a sieve. They cannot choose for us, but we cannot choose without them; and our life is choice.

CHAPTER VII

THE WIND HARP

Metaphysics and poetry and 'facts of mind', that is, accounts of all the strange phantasms that ever possessed 'your philosophy'; dreamers from Thoth the Egyptian to Taylor the English pagan, are my darling studies.—*Letter to Thelwall*, 1796.

> And strange to tell, among that Earthen Lot
> Some could articulate, while others not:
> And suddenly one more impatient cried—
> " Who is the Potter, pray, and who the Pot? "
>
> OMAR KHAYYÁM.

Thus is the Soule, or Spirit of every man all the World to him. The world with all Varietie of things in it, his own body with all it's parts, & changes are himselfe, his own Soule, or Spirit springing up from it's owne ffountaine within itselfe into all those fformes, & Images of things, which it seeth, heareth, smelleth, tasts, feeles, imagineth, or understandeth. . . . In it's lower, & more outward part, which is still itselfe, and within itselfe, it bringeth forth itselfe sportingly into a shadowie ffigure of itselfe and in this shadowie ffigure into innumerable shadowes, & ffigures of those glorious fformes in its superior part. This shadowie ffigure is that, which wee call this world, & the body. The Soule often looking upon this, like Narcissus upon his owne fface in the ffountaine, forgets it to be itselfe, forgets that itselfe is the fface, the shadow, & the ffountaine, so it falls into a fond Love of itselfe in it's owne shadowie ffigure of itselfe. So it languisheth, & dys becoming only a Shadow of itselfe, in which itselfe with all it's superior, and true Glories ly buried (Peter Sterry, *Of the Nature of a Spirit*. See V. de S. Pinto, *Peter Sterry, Puritan and Platonist*, p. 161).

I PASS now from Imagination as a 'fact of mind' to the two doctrines which Coleridge (and Wordsworth) at times drew from it as to a life in or behind Nature. But before discussing this problem, it is well to realize its scope. It has too often been taken as the mere reflection of a taste for certain types of scenery and for impressions from dawn and evening spectacles in the waste. It goes, of course, infinitely beyond this. Any semblance of any life of any kind behind or in the seeming inorganic is within its range. We must include with the visions, which, unfairly to Wordsworth, we tend to think of as comforting and reassuring only, the disconsolate perceptions of Hardy—whether we like to describe him as 'Wordsworth a hundred years older and wiser' or not.

To set beside one another,

> Far and wide the clouds were touched,
> And in their silent faces could he read
> Unutterable love,

and

> Should that morn come, and show thy opened eyes
> All that Life's palpitating tissues feel,
> How wilt thou bear thyself in thy surprise?—
>
> Wilt thou destroy, in one wild shock of shame,
> Thy whole high heaving firmamental frame,
> Or patiently adjust, amend, and heal?

or

> And all the phantom, Nature, stands—
> With all her music in her tone
> A hollow echo of my own—
> A hollow form with empty hands.

is a short way of raising the most comprehensive problem of philosophy.

But in doing so, in making this use of them, we wrench the passages from their original and proper functions. The study of this wrenching, of the translation of imaginative acts into doctrines, is that mode of tracing the source of philosophy in 'facts of mind', which, in Coleridge's view of 1801, was to make the theory of poetry 'supersede all the books of metaphysics and all the books of morals too'.

The difficulty of this study is in preventing our attention straying from utterances as facts of mind to something else—the supposed states of affairs which we take them to be utterances about. To say something, to represent some supposed state of affairs, is *one* function of language—an important but not exclusive function. Our habit is (and it has all the forces that have led to the development of language behind it) to attend to 'what is being said' rather than to 'the saying of it'. This last, the speech-act, is a larger and more complex whole. It includes 'what is being said', it *is* a representation of a supposed state of affairs—to which, if it is a true representation, something else not in the speech-act will correspond and if false, not—but it includes also much more. And it represents (in a slightly different sense, introducing so a second sense of *true*) much more—the history of the speaker's mind, and his feelings and attitudes in the moment of speaking, and conditions of their governance in the future.

If we fix our attention on 'what is being said', the utterance becomes doctrine, doctrine justifying (or not) such and such feelings, doctrine in accord (or not) with such and such facts or other doctrines, doctrine meriting assent, or corrigible in such and such ways. If it is general doctrine, it is to be dealt with in some book of metaphysics or morals. But take the utterance the other way, more comprehensively, as a fact of mind, and in the examination of its structure and functions we shall be at work on the theory of poetry.

Coleridge, I have suggested, very soon left the theory of poetry to become metaphysician and moralist. He returned to it intermittently with extraordinary success; but his exploits as a metaphysician have heavily obscured his work on poetry. Two doctrines in particular concerning the intercourse of the mind with Nature—the doctrines alluded to above in Chapter II—have distracted attention from his conception of the poetic activity. These doctrines are of a lofty and exciting order. Either of them, if true, would be of immense importance. Even if not true, as 'facts of mind' they have already been major influences in the history of poetry; and, if reinterpreted as doctrine and thus modified as facts of mind, they can again become a new and needed motive in poetry. But they cannot be so modified without restoring the connection, which has been broken, between them and Coleridge's conception of language and the imaginative process. I have to dissent then from Miss Powell's opinion, on page 135 of *The Romantic Theory of Poetry*, that Coleridge "confused his interpretation of artistic unity by an attempt to associate it with his 'seminal principle' (of Imagination)". I hope to show that these doctrines derive from that principle. One at least of them started, for Coleridge, from it; in later minds, and, at times, in Coleridge's own mind, they broke loose to become independent doctrines. And yet, in the instances of Imagination which create them, they become concretely one.

The two doctrines can be stated as follows:

1. The mind of the poet at moments, penetrating 'the film of familiarity and selfish solicitude', gains an insight into reality, reads Nature as a symbol of something behind or within Nature not ordinarily perceived.

2. The mind of the poet creates a Nature into which his own feelings, his aspirations and apprehensions, are projected.[1]

In the first doctrine man, through Nature, is linked with something other than himself which he perceives through her. In the second, he makes of her, as with a mirror, a transformed image of his own being.

There are many modes of stating these doctrines. Coleridge and Wordsworth, with their commentators, supply scores of alternative formulations, and the discussion has turned less upon the question: Which of the two was Coleridge's, which Wordsworth's belief? than upon: What is perceived, if not man? To Coleridge, says Shawcross, "the beautiful

---

[1] It is worth remarking that the problem: do we see a table, or do we construct one from sense-experiences? is, formally, the same as this. Cf. p. 55.

in nature was necessarily regarded as symbolic of a spiritual reality, but not co-existent with it, nor yet an essential medium to its fruition" (*B. L.*, I, xix; cf. also pp. xxxv, xxxi). Wordsworth, on the other hand, is usually taken as holding a more pantheistic belief: "Like Hartleism, Spinozism was for Coleridge a temporary phase of belief, but its influence persisted in Wordsworth, until the timid orthodoxy of his middle age glossed it over; it is far more conspicuous in the early draft of *The Prelude*, Wordsworth's Nature is much more than a language, more even than a divine language" (A. E. Powell, *The Romantic Theory of Poetry*, p. 131). But pantheism and theism alike are variants of the realist doctrine.

Miss Powell's able, just and discerning book contains the best attempt that I know to decide by the evidence that other question: Which of these doctrines, the realist or the projective, did either Coleridge or Wordsworth hold? Her attempt seems to me to bring into startling prominence two questions which are prior to this: (1) Are these doctrines necessarily in opposition to one another? (2) What is the relation of any such doctrine to the fact of mind from which it derives? The two questions are evidently not separable. I hope, by examining them, to make more acceptable to some the position that the realist and the projective doctrines are—in the only interpretations in which either is true—both true. As currently formulated they undoubtedly seem to conflict, to be exclusive alternatives. I shall suggest that this appearance is the result of systematic linguistic illusions, arising in the course of the translation *from* the fact of mind *into* philosophic terminologies; that in the forms in which they conflict they are both false; and that in the forms in which they are true they combine to be a description of the fact of mind which is their ground and origin.

With this, of course, *true* has become the prime occasion for misunderstanding and dispute. Its senses are many;[1] and to ask just which of them are relevant is simply to inquire into the whole problem over again under another guise. But this may be convenient here as an indication: that to ask "Is this so?" of "A man is an immortal spirit," "Two and three are five," and "Water freezes at 32° F." is to ask three quite distinct types of question, as we may see by considering what steps would be appropriate in answering them. In the senses in which we will agree that the second and third are true, it would be nonsense to say that the first is. We have neither made man immortal by definition and tautology, nor have we established his immortality by experimental measurement. Similarly with the two doctrines I am here considering. They are neither consequences of *a priori* decisions, nor verifiable as the empirical statements of the

---

[1] I have tabulated some of them in *Mencius on the Mind*, pp. 111-15, and discussed some of the major ambiguities of *true* in *Principles of Literary Criticism*, ch. xxxiii.-v., and the parallel problems of *belief* in *Practical Criticism*, pp. 271-78, and in *Science and Poetry*, ch. vi. Also, more compendiously, in *Basic Rules of Reason*.

sciences are verifiable; and all verifiable statements
are independent of them. But this does not diminish
in the least their interest, or that of the other senses
in which they may be true.

The extraordinary ambiguity, as between these
two doctrines, of nearly all Coleridge's and Wordsworth's utterances of them is the first point to notice.
Miss Powell, in urging that Coleridge held the first
and Wordsworth the second, cites passages from both
that may equally be read either way.

From *The Æolian Harp* (1795):

> O the one Life within us and abroad,
> Which meets all motion and becomes its soul,
> A light in sound, a sound-like power in light,
> Rhythm in all thought, and joyance everywhere.
>
> .   .   .   .   .
>
> And what if all of animated nature
> Be but organic Harps diversely framed,
> That tremble into thought, as o'er them sweeps
> Plastic and vast, one intellectual breeze,
> At once the Soul of each, and God of all?

We can, by weighting *all motion, animated nature,
organic* and *thought,* make this more an account of
the birth of the known from the mind than a perception of a transcendent *living* Reality without.
This perhaps is why Coleridge later in the poem
accepts Sara's rebuke to 'such thoughts' as 'dim
and unhallowed':

> Well hast thou said and holily disprais'd
> These shapings of the unregenerate mind;
> Bubbles that glitter as they rise and break
> On vain Philosophy's aye-babbling spring.

and a footnote on atheism shows that Coleridge was troubled by this passage and its relation to feeling through the next seven years. On the other hand, this is from a letter to Thelwall of December 31, 1796:

The passage in your letter respecting your mother affected me greatly. Well, true or false, heaven is a less gloomy idea than annihilation. Dr Beddoes and Dr Darwin think that *Life* is utterly inexplicable, writing as materialists. You, I understand have adopted the idea that it is the result of organized matter acted on by external stimuli. As likely as any other system, but you assume the thing to be proved. The 'capability of being stimulated into sensation' . . . is my definition of animal life. Monro believes in a plastic, immaterial nature, all-pervading.

> And what if all of animated nature
> Be but organic harps, etc.

(By the bye, that is the favourite of *my* poems; do you like it?) Hunter says that the *blood* is the life, which is saying nothing at all; for, if the blood were *life*, it could never be otherwise than life, and to say it is *alive* is saying nothing; and Ferrier believes in a *soul*, like an orthodox churchman. So much for physicians and surgeons! Now as to the metaphysicians. Plato says it is *harmony*. He might as well have said a fiddlestick's end; but I love Plato, his dear *gorgeous* nonsense; and I, *though last not least, I* do not know what to think about it. On the whole, I have rather made up my mind that I am a mere *apparition*, a naked spirit, and that life is, I myself I; which is a mighty clear account of it.

With *The Æolian Harp* we have to compare *Dejection* [1] (April 4, 1802):

> O Wordsworth! we receive but what we give,
> And in our life alone does Nature live:
> Ours is her wedding garment, ours her shroud!
>   And would we ought behold, of higher worth,
> Than that inanimate cold world allowed
> To the poor loveless ever-anxious crowd,
>   Ah! from the soul itself must issue forth
> A light, a glory, a fair luminous cloud
>   Enveloping the Earth—
> And from the soul itself must there be sent
>   A sweet and potent voice, of its own birth,
> Of all sweet sounds the life and element!

'This strong music in the soul', 'this beautiful and beauty-making power' is Joy,[2]

> Joy that ne'er was given,
> Save to the pure, and in their purest hour,
> Life, and Life's effluence, cloud at once and shower.

It is a conditional power, existing only in minds that are open to Nature, free from impediments in their response.

Dejection begins with the same Wind Harp which gave its title and imagery to the other poem. The

---

[1] It seems possible that Coleridge's definition of 'dejection of mind' (Prospectus to *The Friend*, 1809) is a comment on the thought in this poem: 'doubt or disbelief of the moral government of the world, and the grounds and arguments for the religious hopes of human nature.'

[2] E. H. Coleridge, *The Lake Poets in Somerset*, Transactions of the Royal Society of Literature, vol. xx, "He called it joy, meaning thereby not mirth or high spirits, or even happiness, but a consciousness of entire and therefore well being, when the emotional and intellectual faculties are in equipoise." Coleridge's use of this word here is obviously connected with 'the deep power of joy' in *Tintern Abbey*.

two are in fact complementaries. Then (1795) the
harp, the image of the mind, was

> by the desultory breeze caress'd
> Like some coy maid half yielding to her lover.

Now, premonitory to the storm, comes

> the dull sobbing draft, that moans and rakes
> Upon the strings of this Æolian lute,
> Which better far were mute.

And the Joy which, in

> wedding Nature to us, gives in dower
> A new Earth and a new Heaven

is cut off not only by impediments within, but by
afflictions from without:

> each visitation
> Suspends what nature gave me at my birth,
> My shaping spirit of Imagination.

Like the harp, he can give out now no more:

> Such a soft floating witchery of sound
> As twilight Elfins make, when they at eve
> Voyage on gentle gales from Fairyland,
> Where Melodies round honey-dropping flowers,
> Footiess and wild, like birds of Paradise,
> Nor pause, nor perch, hovering on untam'd wing!

but only

> a scream
> Of agony by torture lengthened out.

The 'one intellectual breeze' has become a Mad
Lutanist,

> Thou Actor, perfect in all tragic sounds!
> Thou mighty Poet, e'en to frenzy bold!
> What tell'st thou now about?

But the instrument is disabled. When the wind falls, we may hear the Harp begin to sound to it again:

It tells another tale, with sounds less deep and loud!
  A tale of less affright,
  And tempered with delight,
As thou thyself had framed the tender lay!
  'Tis of a little child
  Upon a lonesome wild,
Not far from home, but she hath lost her way:
And now moans low in bitter grief and fear,
And now screams loud, and hopes to make her mother hear.

As before, we cannot say, if we take the poem as a whole, that it contains the one doctrine rather than the other. The colours of Nature are a suffusion from the light of the mind, but the light of the mind in its turn, the shaping spirit of Imagination, comes from the mind's response to Nature:

  To thee do all things live from pole to pole
  Their life the eddying of thy living soul.

Eddying is one of Coleridge's greatest imaginative triumphs. An eddy is in something, and is a conspicuous example of a balance of forces.

This ambiguity (or rather, completeness) in Coleridge's thought here and his peculiar use of the Wind-Harp image, give us a concrete example of that self-knowledge, which, as we saw in Chapter III, was for him, both 'speculatively and practically', the principle of all his thinking. When, in his poem: *To William Wordsworth, Lines Composed, for the greater part in the night, on which he finished the recitation of his*

Poem (*in thirteen Books*) *concerning the growth and history of his own Mind* (January 7, 1807), Coleridge set down what seemed to him most significant about *The Prelude*, there is the same co-adunation of the two doctrines. *Spirit*, we may recall, was, for Coleridge, a word to which he gave more meaning than perhaps most of his readers do.

> Herein consists the essence of a spirit, that it is self-representative (*B. L.*, I, 184).
> They and they only can acquire the philosophic imagination, the sacred power of self-intuition, who within themselves can interpret and understand the symbol, that the wings of the air-sylph are forming within the skin of the caterpillar. . . . They know and feel, that the *potential* works *in* them, even as the *actual* works on them! In short, all the organs of sense are framed for a corresponding world of sense; and we have it. All the organs of spirit are framed for a correspondent world of spirit: though the latter organs are not developed in all alike. But they exist in all, and their first appearance discloses itself in the *moral* being (*B. L.*, I, 167).

Here are the opening lines:

> O Friend! O Teacher! God's great gift to me!
> Into my heart have I receiv'd that Lay
> More than historic, that prophetic Lay
> Wherein (high theme by Thee first sung aright)
> Of thy own Spirit thou hast lov'd to tell
> What *may* be told, by words revealable;
> With heavenly breathings, like the secret soul
> Of vernal growth, oft quickening in the heart,
> Thoughts that obey no mastery of words,
> Pure self-beholdings! Theme hard as high!

Of *smiles* spontaneous, and mysterious *fears*
(The first-born they of Reason and twin-birth),
Of tides obedient to external force,
And currents self-determined, as might seem,
Or by some inner Power; of moments awful,
Now in thy inner life, and now abroad,
When power streamed from thee, and thy soul received
The light reflected, as a light bestowed.

At first sight this may seem to decide definitely
for the projective doctrine of the mind as the source
of any light it finds in Nature; but the last lines
are not to be separated from the earlier. The
'moments awful' are not separable from the 'tides
obedient to external force', and with the 'currents
self-determined as might seem' the image of the
'eddying of thy living soul' is not far away.

Coleridge was to Wordsworth

The most intense of Nature's worshippers
In many things my Brother, chiefly here
In this my deep devotion.

If we turn now to Wordsworth's own descriptions
of the mind's intercourse with Nature, we shall
find less of this double vision. His is a less microscopic view; he is more interested in the products
than in the process, and when he notes the process
is not concerned to analyse it. And this was a
source of his success. When Miss Powell writes,
"Though Wordsworth, more than Coleridge, recognized the subjective nature of his vision," I feel
impelled to dissent; but when she continues, "the
result is far more objectified. The poems of Coleridge (mostly early) which are inspired by this

conception of Nature leave us with the idea of his emotional experience; those of Wordsworth, with a mental picture of a scene or a human form," [1] the distinction seems to me perfectly just. But the very fact that Wordsworth more projected (objectified) his vision, makes him more apt to write as though he were not aware of its source in himself. It may be true, as Miss Powell says, that "though he recognizes a marvellous fitness for human expression in Nature, he never loses sight of the fact that man recreates and moulds forms to make them express his feeling" (p. 141). As a matter of conscious theory he may never, in his earlier years, have accepted the realist view. But he often writes as though it were otherwise:

> Far and wide the clouds were touched,
> And in their silent faces could he read
> Unutterable love.   (*Excursion*, I, 203.)

> The sick sight
> And giddy prospect of the raving stream,
> The unfettered clouds, and region of the Heavens,
> Tumult and peace, the darkness and the light
> Were all like workings of one mind, the features
> Of the same face, blossoms upon one tree.
>   (*The Prelude*, VI, 564.)

And, in the most famous example, when

> we are laid asleep
> In body, and become a living soul;
> While with an eye made quiet by the power
> Of harmony, and the deep power of joy,
> We see into the life of things,

---

[1] *The Romantic Theory of Poetry*, p. 144.

it is not easy to suppose (though he contemplates the possibility that this is 'a vain belief' in the next line) that to Wordsworth here 'the life of things' is 'a life lent from the poet's own spirit' or that 'the mystery of Nature for Wordsworth is not that she links him to something beyond himself, but that she gives concrete shape to his noblest aspirations', as Miss Powell writes on p. 140.

But my point here does not concern Wordsworth's beliefs (a question, in this case, of biographical rather than critical importance), but a much more fundamental matter: namely the puzzling ambiguity of these utterances. Miss Powell herself illustrates the remark I have just cited with,

> the forms
> Of Nature have a passion in themselves,
> That intermingles with those works of man.
> (*Prelude*, XII, 290.)

overlooking, apparently, the contradiction. If Nature does not link him to something beyond himself, the passions which the forms of Nature *have in themselves* must be an investment from the poet's spirit. A fine opportunity for a logical rough-house thus presents itself. It is better though to attempt to trace some of the ambiguities [1] which give rise to it.

---

[1] I am considering here only some chief members of the Western nineteenth-century group of *Natures*. If we took account of Western senses in general—still more if we included Indian and Chinese conceptions—a vastly more intricate and more diverse collection would require treatment. That we continue to ignore all but relatively parochial meanings here, in a world which is manifestly

Nature, evidently, all through this discussion has been multiply ambiguous. Its chief senses here seem to be these:

I. The influences, of whatever kind, to which the mind is subject from whatever is without and independent of itself.

II. Those 'images', 'figments', 'things', 'existences' or 'realities', which, through the perceptive and imaginative activities of the mind (in response to I), we take to be the world in which we live.

closing—almost weekly—into one (at present, self-destructive) society, is evidence chiefly of our inadequate technique in comparative studies. It is with pleasure, therefore, that I cite here—in a footnote whose length will ensure it prominence—an extremely able summary, by Professor R. D. Jameson of Tsing Hua University, Peking, of some main differences between western and Chinese conceptions of Nature. (See *Chinese Social and Political Science Review*, vol. xvii, No. 4, January 1934.)

"There is a difference of opinion between China and the West as to the nature of nature and the definition of fact. Mencius and the civilization he represents, having returned adequate answers to the questions which historically have been put to them, are interested in 'that wonderful, vain, diverse and wavering subject,' or, to use the words of Mencius, in ' man's that—wherein differs from birds-beasts, that small-light,' to which the West gives the name ' human nature ' and China the name *hsing*. This, for Mencius and his associates, is the frame within which thought operates and gives facts their factiousness. In the Western tradition physical nature is thought to supply the frame to which man makes the attempt to adapt himself. Many limitations must be placed on this contention, which has been presented in an exaggerated form to make the difference obvious. Yet, if this rough distinction is acceptable as a general difference, it should become clear that the Chinese world is incomprehensible to the Westerner; for the Westerner is in the habit of asking, in Western terms, Is this natural? and the Chinese of asking, Is it human? The Western ethic tends to find its sanction in biology, the Chinese in tradition."

The importance of the issues raised, and their interest even in the Western field of comparative studies will, I hope, win me excuse for quoting here what is part of a review of my *Mencius on the Mind*—a study parallel in some respects to this.

III. A selection of II including only such of them as are perceived by all men alike, allowance being made for variations in the conditions of perception (these last being themselves a selection of III; the typical example would be short-sightedness—departures from normal vision in the short-sighted being fully explicable). This is the world of our practical every-day experience whose laws are verified every minute of our lives.

IV. A still narrower selection from II including only such of them as are required at any stage in the theoretical development of Physics for the purpose of giving an account of Nature in Sense I. A little while ago these were things possessing the primary qualities of matter; recently physics has dispensed with some of them, and Nature, therefore, in Sense IV has ceased to be as material as it used to be. It still, however, in Sense III, remains as material as it was when Dr Johnson, quite pertinently to the discussion as he saw it, was 'striking his foot with mighty force against a large stone, till he rebounded from it' in Harwich Churchyard, by way of refuting Berkeley. For Johnson supposed Berkeley to be arguing that Nature, in Sense III, is not as in all our daily life we know it to be.

However 'immaterial' Physics becomes, it still, as Lenin remarks, "remains a science of matter in the sense that it accepts some objective reality existing independently of the human mind and reflected by it. 'Matter disappears' means that the form of the limit which we have known up to now vanishes, as our knowledge penetrates deeper; those properties of matter which seemed immutable and primary (impenetrability, inertia, mass, etc.) disappear, and now become relative, belonging only to certain states of matter. For the sole 'property of matter'—with the recognition of which materialism is vitally connected—is the property of being *objective reality*, of existing outside our cognition."

(*Materialism and Empirio-Criticism*, 220.)

Physics derives from and verifies itself in the Nature of Sense III—which must always remain *material* in that its laws—exemplified in the fact that if we put our finger in the fire it will be burnt —are of a certain type. No metaphysic has the least effect upon such laws, and upon them our whole existence depends. Thus, in this sense, we can never cease to take a Materialist view of Nature.

In seeming opposition, in *this* discussion, we have Idealist views that may be framed in terms of either of the two doctrines which have been occupying us in this chapter. It is notable that critics commonly describe them both as Idealism, ignoring their difference. By one of them Nature is a language [1] —revealing not ourselves but something else; and to understand the doctrine we must know in what sense we are taking *ourselves*. The other is in terms of Sense II: in imaginative perception we see Nature as invested with characters derived from

[1] On the metaphor employed in this, see the following chapter.

our own feelings, our hopes and fears, desires, and thoughts. Nature, here in Sense II, is a projection of our whole response to Nature in Sense I: it is the music by which the string represents the wind, and thus,

> In our life alone does Nature live.

But, equally,

> that inanimate cold world allowed
> To the poor loveless ever-anxious crowd,

or Nature in Sense III, is as it is perceived by us. Apart from the response of the organism to Nature in Sense I, there is no Nature in Sense II. As Coleridge put it, sensation, which to Hobbes or Hartley supplied data from which all the rest was to be built up, "is itself but vision nascent, not the cause of intelligence, but intelligence itself revealed as an earlier power in the process of self-construction" (*B. L.* I, 187). However we restrict (or expand) our view of Nature, it remains *our view.* What sensation gives us is only by a weak metaphor *given* to us. He writes to Wordsworth in 1815 on the philosophic poem he hoped Wordsworth would have written, "I supposed you first to have meditated the faculties of man in the abstract, *in their correspondence with his sphere of action, and, first in the feeling, touch and taste, then in the eye and lastly in the ear*—to have laid a solid and immovable foundation for the edifice by removing the sandy sophisms of Locke, and the mechanic dogmatists, and demonstrating that *the senses were living growths and develop-*

ments of the mind and spirit, in a much juster as well as a higher sense, than the mind can be said to be formed by the senses."

I have italicized here the phrases which need our closest attention: the order in which Coleridge mentions the senses is significant. It is with feeling (muscular resistance), touch and taste that we are most likely to suppose that the qualities we perceive in Nature belong to her in her own right and apart from our perception of them. And it is with sounds that we are least so tempted. We are willing enough to think that Nature, if there were no ears, would be silent; less willing to think that, if there were no eyes, she would be colourless; and very obstinately loath to admit that without skins and muscles there would be no bodies. But for any account of perception which is not demonstrably incomplete, all the sensory qualities of Nature (Sense II) arise only in the interaction of Nature (Sense I) with perceiving organisms. The most elementary components of perception are already responses, and responses moreover whose form has a prehuman origin.[1]

Nature, then, even in Senses III and IV, even when all the reflections from our perceiving activity that can be eliminated have been eliminated, remains radically a production of our perceptions.

---

[1] " Nature has been projected in organic history as an Object in contrast with a Subject; but for the human individual it is preformed, or prepared for, in his inherited organization; for the organic growth of perceptions in the mind corresponds to the growth of the nervous system " (Carveth Read, *The Metaphysics of Nature*, 125).

In terms of such a multiple definition the gap between the two doctrines—that the mind can see God in or through Nature, and that it can only see itself projected—becomes an artificial product of a shifting [1] of the senses of *Nature, mind,* and *see.* A fuller description of the 'facts of mind' from which the poet and the philosopher alike set out carries both doctrines as accordant functions, as uncontradictory interpretations. But to accept this we must disallow the transformations that inevitably occur in deriving the doctrines from the 'facts of mind'. And it is better not to say (as I have just said) that a fuller *description* of the facts of mind yields the doctrines. For any description in prose is itself a doctrine hard to keep from being just one or other of the two we are considering. The antinomy between them then seems to be 'solved' merely by electing for one of them. It is better to say, with Coleridge, that our concern is with the fact of mind itself, the immediate self-consciousness in the imaginative moment which is the source of the doctrines; and again that it is not the doctrines, abstractly considered, that we have to discuss but the originative facts of mind they (sometimes only, alas) express, that we have to know or be. "Every object," said Aristotle, "is best viewed when that which is not separate is posited in separation, as is

[1] Since any account of these shifts must itself use positions, the gap will reappear as between various accounts of these. To suppose otherwise is like hoping to see all things on all their sides from one viewpoint. The gap we cannot escape, but we can recognize it, in its various places, as a necessary, not an accidental defect in the treatment of a whole by a part.

done by the arithmetician." But this is the supreme exception. Positing, in separation, that which is not separate is the source of all metaphysical difficulties here—which is to say, of all metaphysics.

I shall therefore close this chapter with the warning that, in going on to consider Coleridge's other approaches to, and recessions from, this position, we shall find him and ourselves slipping—through the treacheries of abstract language—into positions in which we can no longer know that coalescence of the two doctrines which the Wind Harp image can achieve. It is the privilege of poetry to preserve us from mistaking our notions either for things or for ourselves. Poetry is the completest mode of utterance.

CHAPTER VIII

THE BOUNDARIES OF THE MYTHICAL

> Into blind darkness enter they
> That worship ignorance;
> Into darkness, as it were, greater
> They that delight in knowledge.
> Other, indeed, they say, than knowledge!
> Other, they say, than non-knowledge!
> Thus have we heard from the wise
> Who to us explained It.
>
> *Īśā Upanishad.*

THE Imagination projects the life of the mind not upon Nature in Sense I, the field of the influences from without to which we are subject, but upon a Nature that is already a projection of our sensibility. The deadest Nature that we can conceive is already a Nature of our making. It is a Nature shaped by certain of our needs, and when we 'lend to it a life drawn from the human spirit' it is reshaped in accordance with our other needs. But our needs do not originate in us. They come from our relations to Nature in Sense I. We do not create the food that we eat, or the air that we breathe, or the other people we talk to; we do create, from our relations to them, every image we have 'of' [1] them. *Image* here is a betraying and unsatisfactory word; it

---

[1] This 'of' here is the 'of' of apposition. A similar sentence with the 'of' of reference would belong to a discussion of a very different topic, the ordering of knowledge *within* Nature in Senses II and III.

suggests that these images, with which all that we
can know is composed, are in some way insub-
stantial or unreal, mere copies of actualities other
than themselves—figments. But *figment* and *real* and
substantial are themselves words with no meaning
that is not drawn from our experience. To say of
anything that it is a figment seems to presuppose
things more real than itself; but there is nothing
within our knowledge more real than these images
To say that anything is an image suggests that there
is something else to which it corresponds; but here
all correspondence is between images. In short, the
notion of reality derives from comparison between
images, and to apply it as between images and
things that are not images is an illegitimate ex-
tension which makes nonsense of it.

This deceiving practice is an example of that
process of abstraction which makes it almost inevitable that the two doctrines discussed in the last
chapter—the projective and the realist doctrines
of the life in Nature—should be conceived as
contradictory. "If projected, not real; if real, not
projected", we shall say, unless we are careful to
recall that the meanings of *real* and *projected* derive
from the imaginative fact of mind, and that when
they are thus put in opposition they are products
of abstraction and are useful only for other purposes
than the comprehension of the fact of mind.

As such abstractions they induce further facts of
mind—apprehensions of them as *theories* or *beliefs*—
and these, as Coleridge's own history shows, can

become gross obstacles to the return of 'the philosophic imagination, the sacred power of self-intuition'. Taken as contradictory theories, they encourage very different attitudes to the opportunities of life. Coleridge, as 'the years matured the silent strife', became more and more held by attitudes consonant with the Realist doctrine, less and less able to recover his earlier integral vision of the poet's mind. But the feeling that whatever he had to say was half the truth, that there was another half, irreconcilable but equally required, haunted him. It is behind his accounts of Reason: "Plato's works are preparatory exercises for the mind. He leads you to see that propositions involving in themselves contradictory conceptions are nevertheless true; and which, therefore, must belong to a higher logic—that of ideas." "This is the test of a truth so affirmed (a truth of the reason, an Idea) that in its own proper form it is *inconceivable*. . . . And here we have a second test and sign of a truth so affirmed, that it can come forth out of the moulds of the understanding only in the disguise of two contradictory conceptions." [1]

This is 'dangerous thought' as Hegel, for example, has shown; an analysis of the meanings which seem to be contradictory is a better prescription; but the passage shows, in the very desperateness of the suggested remedy, Coleridge's sense that some-

---

[1] See *Table Talk*, April 30, 1830. The extraordinary balance of Coleridge's mind is well seen in his comments on animal magnetism to be found under the same date. In Plato, see e.g. *Republic*, 523.

thing was lacking. And his struggles between Being and Knowing as the fundamental form of self-consciousness show it too.

"For to us, self-consciousness is not a kind of *being*, but a kind of *knowing*, and that too the highest and farthest that exists for us" (*B. L.*, I, 187, 1816).

This elevation of the spirit above the semblances of custom and the senses to a world of spirit, this life in the idea, even in the supreme and Godlike, which alone merits the name of life, and without which our organic life is but a state of somnambulism; this it is which affords the sole anchorage in the storm, and at the same time the substantiating principle of all true wisdom, the satisfactory solution of all the contradictions of human nature, of the whole riddle of the world. This alone belongs to and speaks intelligibly to all alike, the learned and the ignorant, if but the heart listens. For alike present in all, it may be awakened but it cannot be given. *But let it not be supposed, that it is a sort of knowledge: No! it is a form of being, or indeed it is the only knowledge that truly is, and all other science is real only as far as it is symbolical of this.* The material universe, saith a Greek philosopher, is but one vast complex mythus (*i.e.* symbolical representation); and mythology the apex and complement of all genuine physiology. But as this principle cannot be implanted by the discipline of logic, so neither can it be excited or evolved by the arts of rhetoric. For it is an immutable truth, that what comes from the heart, that alone goes to the heart; what proceeds from a Divine impulse, that the Godlike alone can awaken (*The Friend*, Section 2, Essay 11, 1818).

'Read this over until you understand it. God bless you!' Coleridge might have added this at the end of many of his best paragraphs. For they have not been understood when they have been read merely as pious exhortations. Behind them was the experience of the imaginative moment. And it is this which 'speaks intelligibly to all alike if but the heart listens'.

Another name for the heart is *feeling*, a word which, especially in the plural, has often to-day a derogatory tinge and is associated with vagueness and sentimentality. It may be supposed, however, that if Coleridge gave it an important place in his teaching, it had an interesting meaning. And he did give it an enormously important place. "My opinion is that deep thinking is attainable only by a man of deep feeling . . . and all truth is a species of revelation" (*Letter to Poole*, March 23, 1801). "I hold that association depends in a much greater degree on the recurrence of states of feeling than on trains of ideas. . . . Believe me, Southey! a metaphysical solution, that does not *tell* you something in the heart is grievously to be suspected as apocryphal. I almost think that ideas *never* recall ideas, as far as they are ideas, any more than leaves in a forest create each other's motion. The breeze it is that runs through them—it is the soul, the state of feeling" (*To Southey*, Aug. 7, 1803).

What then is feeling? It is here Coleridge's name for all those factors in the mind's response to Nature (Sense I) which are cut out as we pass from Nature in Sense II to Nature in Sense III. He uses it in other senses: as the flavour or tinge of an emotional experience, as the sense of touch, as a general collecting term for all distinguishable ingredients of experience; but in its most important use, it stands for all these motions in the mind by which the projected objects of our perceptions and thoughts are invested with more characters than those required in the administration of practical affairs. This way of describing feeling attempts to set a boundary around practical affairs, and the perceptions sufficient for them, which cannot, of course, in fact be drawn. The real problem would be to say into what perceptions feelings do not enter. But we can distinguish affairs in which our feelings about them are relevant from those in which they are not. We applaud the surgeon, for example, for keeping his feelings out of his perceptions. And this *relevance*—which is, of course, a mere reference to our purposes as a whole—gives the essential line of division. In the conduct of our lives we sometimes need perceptions into which our hopes and fears and desires enter as little as possible. These are the perceptions sought by the man of science. They result in a Nature, over which our power of control is increasing with embarrassing leaps and bounds. And through this Nature (the world of natural science) it will soon be *possible* for us to remove most of the physical ills that oppress humanity. But to turn this possibility into an actuality we need wisdom, which natural science in itself cannot give us. For wisdom requires a different co-ordination of our perceptions, yielding another Nature for us to live in—a Nature in which our hopes and fears and desires, by projection, can come to terms with one another. It is this Nature that 'comes from the heart, that alone goes to the heart'. It is such a Nature that the religions in the past have attempted to provide for man. And it is with such a Nature that the political mythologizing of the more cramped sections of humanity—a Nature including Nordic destinies and Japanese 'missions' —did endeavour to direct world affairs.

We live, to-day, half in and half out of two projected Natures. One is a Nature in Sense III, confused, through lack of reflection, with the unprojected ingressive Nature of Sense I. The other is a Nature in Sense II—shot through and through with our feelings and thus a mythology for them. These two Natures are at war. The enormous development in our conception of Nature in Senses III and IV by seeming to threaten the sanctions of these projected feelings, is making them sickly, exaggerated and hysterical. We feel increasingly cut off from every aspect of the world in which it seems in significant connection with ourselves. We are losing our 'intimacy with the very spirit which gives the physiognomic expression to all the works of nature'. And to lose touch with Nature here is to lose touch with ourselves. From the other side the interferences of mythology with science in the past have left an enmity. To the world of natural science, other mythology seems gross imposture: and in reply this other mythology either belittles science or frames itself anew in abstract concepts which can no longer 'speak intelligibly to all alike', and to which the heart cannot listen.

These evils are familiar and their grounds go deep. It is not to be supposed that any mere improvement in philosophic theory will remedy them. Indeed the first effect of inquiries is to sharpen them.

A view which alleges that they are unnecessary, that with more self-knowledge we could live in a world which was *both* a transcription of our practical needs for exact prediction and accommodation, *and* a mythology adequate to the whole of our spiritual life, meets with attack from both sides. It is accused of recommending make-belief on one hand, and of heresy or blasphemy on the other.

Answers can, of course, be given to both charges. But no answer will meet them unless it can induce a return to the 'self-realizing intuition' from which any answer must come. And argument is not the mode of inducing this. However, here are some parts of such answers.

Make-belief is an enervating exercise of fancy not to be confused with imaginative growth. The saner and greater mythologies are not fancies; they are the utterance of the whole soul of man and, as such, inexhaustible to meditation. They are no amusement or diversion to be sought as a relaxation and an escape from the hard realities of life. They are these hard realities in projection, their symbolic recognition, co-ordination and acceptance. Through such mythologies our will is collected, our powers unified, our growth controlled. Through them the infinitely divergent strayings of our being are brought into 'balance or reconciliation'. The 'opposite and discordant qualities' of things in them acquire a form; and such integrity as we possess as 'civilized' men is our inheritance through them. Without his mythologies man is only a cruel animal without a soul—for a soul is a central part of his governing mythology—he is a congeries of possibilities without order and without aim.

He has paid for them, of course. The imagination, the coadunating, mythopœic power can break loose from 'the activity of thought and the vivacity of the accumulative memory'. "If the check of the senses and the reason were withdrawn imagination would become mania." "When a man mistakes his thoughts for persons and things, he is mad. A madman is properly so defined" (*Table Talk*, July 25, 1832). Man has often been mad. "The development of the imagination in primitive man had certain disastrous consequences, moral and speculative. It encroached upon the objectivity of Nature and often left its victim less intelligent than an unembarrassed ape" (Carveth Read, *The Metaphysics of Nature*, p. 328). It can do so still. We seem likely to see whole nations again in the control of such madmen, as they have been in the past. And if these myths usually destroy their creators, it is not until they have destroyed much else.

> Lo! which a greet thyng is affeccioun!
> Men may dye of imaginacioun,
> So depe may impressioun be take.

Coleridge can hardly have realized the immense consequences of this definition: [1] we must not read it too strictly or we would all be mad. We all mistake our thoughts for persons and things in some degree. And those in charge of the organized traditional mythologies of most peoples expressly encourage these mistakes and indeed officially insist that they be made. But those who *believe* any myth in the sense of *acting in all respects according to it* are rare and abnormal people. We do not regard even these as mad unless their myths are very disjointed, or incompatible with continued existence, or morally contrary to the communal or traditional myths. We are more likely to regard them, after a time, as saints.

Most men who believe their myths do so in a very restricted sense, with qualifications, both as to the occasions on which the myth is operant at all and as to its influence on their conduct, that are extremely intricate. And these qualifications evidently vary from myth to myth and from man to man. It will be seen that I am taking *Belief* here as Accordant Action; and *Action* then must be taken in its widest possible sense. It includes intellectual assent, feeling, submission in desire, attitude and will—all modes of response to the myth from mere contemplation to overt behaviour. In this sense, the remark that most belief is severely limited, is obviously true. Universal *complete* belief, for example, in Buddhism or Christianity would bring the human race to an

[1] But see the allegory in the First Essay in *The Friend*.

end with one generation. And yet complete belief is often the aim officially set before the believer.

What Coleridge called Good Sense, or Sanity, the recognition of a wider field of human purposes, intervenes to correct the exorbitant claims of any one myth. If every myth is a projection of some human situation, of some co-ordination of human feelings, needs and desires, the scope of its relevance and therefore of its proper influence upon action must be limited. If the situation which gives rise to the myth changes, if, for example, through the development of science (that specialized type of myth) man becomes no longer helplessly subject to infinite uncontrollable disaster, a part of the sanction of other myths is removed. But it will not have been our theoretical knowledge of Nature in Sense III that has discredited these myths. It will have been the results of the power given us by that knowledge, our changed situation and the changes in our feelings that ensue.

Other myths do not derive from knowledge in the sense in which science is knowledge; though to suppose that they do and thus to take them as giving us knowledge, in this sense, in return, is the chief human failing, the process to which Coleridge should have pointed in his definition of madness. For the claim to be knowledge, in this sense, is the claim to unrestricted control over the anticipation of events. What we know, as science, that we must act upon, under pain of imminent danger to our lives if we do not. I am not speaking, of course, of theoretical or philosophic physics (which only the experimentalist in his laboratory can act upon), but of those laws of Nature (Sense III) which are verified in all our experience every minute. We step out of the way of the oncoming motor-bus. But our response to poetry is restricted and conditional. What has gone into it determines what we may properly and wisely take from it. 'We receive but what we give.' If we try to take more from the myth than has gone into it we violate the order of our lives.

Thus for every myth, from the largest cosmic drama to the least and most fleeting act of the poetic imagination—the lover's grass that sighs (see p. 30)—there is a range of relevance for our response to it which is set ultimately by its origin in the mind. Not, of course, in the mind of its original maker (when it had one maker), but in whatever mind entertains (or recreates) it. We must add though some phrase like Coleridge's 'in so far as it is representative of the human mind in general' as a control against individual aberrations. But we need a still stronger control than this. For, if, as I have been suggesting, an extremely general misunderstanding and misuse of myth and a confusion of it with the special myths of science, has been characteristic of humanity, a mere appeal to the 'all in each of all men' is not sufficient. We have to go a step further, and appeal to an ideal of sanity or integrity or sincerity in the mind, to its growing order in response to the Universe (Nature, Sense I).

I have been taking the largest and the smallest myths together. It is of assistance to realize that the discussion applies as much to our perception of other minds as to the projection of a cosmic life into Nature. The peculiar merits which lovers discern in one another, and the special virtues with which fellow-nationals are invested have their origin evidently in feeling. Probably the application of my remarks to the larger myths will have most occupied the reader. But an account of the origin and function of myths is more conveniently tested on lesser examples. Any collection of interpretations [1] of almost any poem will show enough mistakes in the use of myths to illustrate the points I have been labouring. Coleridge's discussion of 'Thou best philosopher' (p. 132 above) is, I think, a fair example. But the restriction of the myth's relevance to what has gone into it, and thus the derivative contrast between poetic myth and science or history, is perfectly plain in all respectable reading. No one, for example, thinks the worse of Shakespeare for saying that Beauty and Truth vanished from the earth with his Phœnix and Turtle. And few who read the poem closely will suppose that it is any less serious for being a poetic, not a scientific, myth.

On such ground, with such minor myths, I am not in much fear that the theory of the projective imagination will meet with dissent from those who understand it. Poetry is full of minor myths which

---

[1] Specimens, if required, will be found in my *Practical Criticism* and in " Fifteen Lines of Landor ", *The Criterion*, April 1933.

are managed without the embarrassments of confusion with statements about matters of fact, and
without the uneasiness that comes from doubt as
to their sanction. So far as what I have said is
taken as applying to these myths only, I am likely
to have seemed to be setting forth the obvious.
But dissent is not merely probable but certain if
this account is applied to all myths, or—to put it
the other way—if *all* views of Nature are taken to
be projections of the mind, and the religions as well
as science are included among myths.

To such dissent, from whatever angle it comes,
those to whom such an account recommends itself
as consonant with their experience, will inevitably
adopt a diagnostic attitude, an attitude that must
seem, equally inevitably, discourteous and even
insulting to the dissenters. But any view which
pretends to be a world-view must do so. It must
be interested not in refuting other views but in
tracing the causes of their distortions. And, with
this apology, I will consider briefly some typical
objections. A cause which is common to perhaps
all cases of dissent has its incidence in the process
by which experience gives place to doctrine. Coleridge sometimes wrote very clearly on this point,
though his best passages are interwoven with much
that I should describe as highly confused dissent.

The groundwork, therefore, of all true philosophy
is the full apprehension of the difference between the
contemplation of reason, namely, that intuition of
things which arises when we possess ourselves, as one

with the whole, which is substantial knowledge, and that which presents itself when transferring reality to the negations of reality, to the ever-varying framework of the uniform life, we think of ourselves as separated beings, and place nature in antithesis to the mind, as object to subject, thing to thought, death to life. This is abstract knowledge, or the science of the mere understanding . . . which leads to a science of delusion then only when it would exist for itself instead of being the instrument of the former (that intuition of things which arises when we possess ourselves as one with the whole)— instead of being, as it were, a translation of the living word into a dead language, for the purposes of memory, arrangement, and general communication (*The Friend*, Sect. 2, Essay 11).

We may add, the purposes of calculation, and of control over our environment. To the man of science who objects to the world, which his science investigates so successfully, being called a myth, it will probably be enough to remark that as he investigates it the picture he frames of it changes, and that it is this changing picture that is the myth. The fundamentally important difference between the myths of natural science and the myths of poetry in the unrestricted claim upon our overt action of the former (getting out of the way of motor-cars, for example) has been insisted on above.

A more rooted objection comes from the other side. A myth which has long been taken as more than a myth—as the representation of a fact independent of our apprehension of it and in no way conditioned by our experience—gains a control over our minds which makes the recognition of it as a myth, as a symbolization of our experience only, often impossible. And here no arguments can be of avail. The terms in which the arguments would have to be conducted are too discrepant, the systems of meanings in the two minds are too diversely organized for useful discussion. And yet even here there is a mode of reconciliation which seems to be illustrated in Coleridge himself. In much of his writing and discourse he was unquestionably *not* treating Christianity as a myth. But the theologian, the philosopher, the scientist and the poet were not at ease together within him. He is a compendium of the separable powers of man's intellect, and it is to be remarked that when they most come into accord in him he speaks with most authority:

> As every faculty, with every the minutest organ of our nature, owes its whole reality and comprehensibility to an existence incomprehensible and groundless, because the ground of all comprehension; not without the union of all that is essential in all the functions of our spirit, not without an emotion tranquil from its very intensity, shall we worthily contemplate in the magnitude and integrity of the world that life-ebullient stream which breaks through every momentary embankment, again, indeed, and evermore to embank itself, but within no banks to stagnate or be imprisoned.
> But here it behoves us to bear in mind, that all true reality has both its ground and its evidence in the will, without which as its complement science itself is but an elaborate game of shadows, begins in abstractions and ends in perplexity. For considered merely intellectually, individuality, as individuality, is only conceivable as with and in the Universal and the Infinite, neither

before nor after it. No transition is possible from one to the other, as from the architect to the house, or the watch to its maker. The finite form can neither be laid hold of, nor is it anything of itself real, but merely an apprehension, a frame-work which the human imagination forms by its own limits, as the foot measures itself on the snow; and the sole truth of which we must again refer to the Divine imagination, in virtue of its omniformity; for even as thou art capable of beholding the transparent air as little during the absence as during the presence of light, so canst thou behold the finite things as actually existing neither with nor without the substance. Not without, for then the forms cease to be, and are lost in night. Not with, for it is the light, the substance shining through it which thou canst alone really see (*The Friend*, Sect. 2, Essay 11).

It was the whole being of man—the Reason [1]—which, for Coleridge, was the eye in this analogy.

> Whene'er the mist, that stands 'twixt God and thee,
> Defecates to a pure transparency
> That intercepts no light and adds no stain—
> There Reason is, and then begins her reign!

But *light*, along with *see*, is here fundamentally ambiguous. It is either Nature in our first sense—all the influences to which the mind is susceptible from without. Or it is our response to those influences—that 'which thou canst alone really see', the vision that arises through the interception of these influences by the whole man. As such a vision it is a myth—'a framework which the human

---

[1] I am aware that Reason was many different things at different times for Coleridge. (See the learned work of René Wellek, *Immanuel Kant in England*, pp. 103–106.) I choose this account as most relevant to his doctrine of Imagination.

imagination forms by its own limits'—the bounding, all-inclusive myth in so far as 'the whole soul of man' is reflected in it. And Coleridge's 'Divine imagination' (the human imagination is 'a repetition in the finite mind of the eternal act of creation in the infinite I AM') is a part of that vision and thus a part of the myth. As the inclusive myth, if it could be not abstractly conceived but concretely imagined, it would contain all meanings. Nature, in Sense I, on the other hand, contains the minimum of meaning. It is the other boundary of the mythical. We can say nothing of it and think nothing of it without producing a myth. It is the whatever it is in which we live: and there we have to leave it; for to say more of it is not to speak of it, but of the modes of our life in it. For us, it *can* be only—but it also *must* be—such that *all* the modes of our life are supported by it.

This is, of course, by no means strange doctrine:

When a man has once seen that every single science, except metaphysics, makes use of fictions, he is apt to conclude that the next step for him is to remove these fictions and substitute the Truth. But if he looked closer he would see that human beings cannot get on without mythology. In science, in politics, in art and religion it will be found and can never be driven out. And, if we confine our attention to science, we must say that there is only one science which can have no hypotheses, and is forbidden to employ any fiction or mythology, and that this science with some reason is suspected of non-existence (F. H. Bradley, *Principles of Logic*, I, 342).

My aim in so touching on Coleridge's theology is to suggest that the interval, for him, between what he supposed to be orthodox Christian belief and his philosophy as the poet of the Wind-harp was sometimes very narrow—no wider than a line. And that whether he took a projective view or a realist view of the Life in Nature depended upon the process of 'translation, as it were, of the living word into a dead language'—the replacement of the whole man, the Reason in him, by the Metaphysician or the Theologian. Both doctrines *equally* (and any doctrine in which we may attempt to combine them) yield us, as doctrines, only objects and are but dead words—'even as all objects (as objects) are essentially fixed and dead'.

And if, in using either literal or metaphoric senses of *word, language, myth, symbol* and the rest, we bear in mind the paradigm of the fluctuations of the word *word*, we shall see why any account we give in these terms will have both projective and realist interpretations. And why in a return to the fact of mind, and growth in it, is the only 'solution' of the metaphysical problem—a 'solution' by reintegration and supersession.

Not to be able to occupy one's self continuously with abstractions without at least falling into the illusion that lends them an independent being, without at least lapsing into what is technically called the hypostasy of abstractions, this is a defect and weakness of the human mind which cannot be taken as characteristic of one particular application of its powers (Gompertz, *Greek Thinkers*).

That is a stage at which the matter is too often left. For what is there, of which we can think or speak, which is not a hypostatized abstraction? To eliminate this 'defect and weakness of the human mind' would be to eliminate the mind itself and all its universes. We may grant that there are vicious as well as virtuous abstractions—abstractions which, in their independent being, are of better or worse service to their fellows. As Coleridge points out, things and notions—like the words to which he compares them—may be living or dead, responsive to the rest of things or not. The word in itself comes to us as a mere undulation; it becomes 'a living word' in and with our interpretation of it; and without this it must be 'as sounds in an unknown language, or as the vision of heaven and earth expanded by the rising sun, which falls but as warmth upon the eyelids of the blind' (*The Friend*, Sect. 2, Essay 11).

When Coleridge, at the end of *The Statesman's Manual* drew up his glossary of philosophic terms, the hierarchy of the partial aspects of the mind's activities closed with:

That which is neither a sensation nor a perception, that which is neither individual (that is a sensible intuition) nor general (that is a conception) which neither refers to outward facts, nor yet is abstracted from the forms of perception contained in the understanding; but which is an educt of the imagination actuated by the pure reason, to which there neither is nor can be an adequate correspondent in the world of the senses;—this and this alone is—an Idea. Whether ideas are regulative only, according to Aristotle and Kant; or likewise constitutive, and one with the power and life of nature, according to Plato and Plotinus (ἐν λόγῳ ζωὴ ἦν και ʼη ζωὴ ἦν τὸ φῶς των ἀνθρώπων) is the highest problem of philosophy, and not part of its nomenclature.[1]

'The imagination actuated by the pure reason' is 'the whole soul of man in activity'. What by and in it we know is certainly not a part of philosophy's nomenclature. But what we *say* about it—whether we say that it is the mode of all our knowledge (ideas are regulative); or that it is what we know (ideas are constitutive)—must be said (thus abstractly) in a vocabulary. And I have tried to make the position acceptable that these rival doctrines here derive from different arrangements of our vocabularies and are only seeming alternatives, that each pressed far enough includes the other, and that the Ultimate Unabstracted and Unrepresentable View that thus results is something we are familiar and at home with in the concrete fact of mind.

If this were so, the problems of criticism would no longer abut, as they so often did for Coleridge, on this problem of Reality; they would be freed for the inexhaustible inquiry into the modes of mythology and their integration 'according to their relative worth and dignity' in the growth of our lives.

---

[1] This last problem " is of living Interest to the Philosopher by Profession alone. Both systems are equally true, if only the former abstain from denying *universally* what is denied individually" (*Letter to J. Gooden*, January 14, 1820).

I may conclude this chapter with a parable from Chuang Tzu:

Intelligence went north and was enjoying himself by the stream of Hsuen (the Mysterious), and climbing the Hill of Yin Pin (the Concealed) when he met Wu Wei Wei (Not doing-speaking) to whom he said:

'By what thoughts, by what meditations may the Tao (the Way) be known? By resting in what, by according with what, may the Tao be approached? By relying on what, by following what, may the Tao be attained?'

To these questions Wu Wei Wei returned no answer, not because he would not but because he could not.

Then Intelligence returned south to the White river and the mount of the Solitary End and there he met Extreme Measures, to whom he put the same questions.

'Ha!' cried Extreme Measures, 'I know, I will tell you.' But just as he was about to speak he forgot what he had to say.

So Intelligence returned to the Palace and asked the Yellow Emperor, who replied:

'By no thoughts, no meditations, may the Tao be known. By resting in nothing, by according with nothing, may the Tao be approached. By relying on nothing, by following nothing may it be attained.'

Then Intelligence said to the Yellow Emperor, 'Now you and I know this; but those two know it not.'

And the Yellow Emperor said, 'Wu Wei Wei is entirely right. Extreme Measures is very near. But you and I are far away. Who knows speaks not, who speaks knows not. Therefore the sage teaches a doctrine which is without words. The Tao cannot be brought within human limits, nor can Virtue be reached by human means. That which does is humaneness; that which wants is righteousness; that which deceives is propriety. Therefore when the Tao is lost we have Virtue; when Virtue is lost we have humaneness; when humaneness is lost we have righteousness; when righteousness is lost we have propriety—for the latter is the blooming of the Tao and the beginning of disorder.'

CHAPTER IX

THE BRIDLE OF PEGASUS

Be not as the horse, or the mule, who have no understanding; whose mouth must be held in with bit and bridle, lest they come near unto thee.—*Psalm* xxxii.

> This same stede shal bere you ever-more
> With-outen harm, til ye be ther yow leste.
>
> .   .   .   .
>
> Of sondry doutes thus they jangle and trete
> As lewed peple demeth comunly
> Of thinges that ben maad more subtilly
> Than they can in her lewedness comprehende;
> They demen gladly to the badder ende.
> *The Squieres Tale.*

MAY I invite attention to a few paragraphs from a representative present-day critic on Wordsworth's doctrine and practice of the interpretation of Nature? They will show us where much current opinion is, in this matter. And they provide a convenient specimen for the study of reading ability.

What claim, for instance, is Wordsworth making for his feelings in these lines, from the *Excursion* ?

> Far and wide the clouds were touched
> And in their silent faces could he read
> Unutterable love. Sound needed none
> Nor any voice of joy: his spirit drank
> The spectacle: sensation, soul, and form,
> All melted into him; they swallowed up
> His animal being; in them did he live
> And by them did he live; they were his life.

> In such access of mind, in such high hour
> Of visitation from the living God,
> Thought was not; in enjoyment it expired.
> No thanks he breathed, he proffered no request:
> Rapt into still communion that transcends
> The imperfect offices of prayer and praise. . . .

These last are daring words and more definite perhaps than any others in Wordsworth, in what they claim. He is not merely equalling, but transcending the offices of prayer and praise. Wordsworth is presumably asking us to take him seriously; and if we take him seriously we cannot let such phrases slip by, all merged in one gush of emotion. And once we are asked to consider a theological issue some elementary questions arise.

First, why is this different from pantheism? Does Wordsworth by any denial of his poetic art or of his joy in things suggest that he is communing with a personal God, entirely distinct from his joy in the clouds: or is God, like the poet Donne, merely preaching to him ' from a cloud, but in none'? Herbert tells us that God is not to be found in stars or clouds or any aspect of nature, but in ' the sweet original joy sprung from Thine eye.'

Again, how are we to know that Wordsworth really felt these very emotions when he looked at the cloud, and that some of them did not rather arrive later when he wrote the poem? And if we pass over this difficulty, it is possible, of course, that the presence, which Wordsworth felt was in the cloud, existed only in his own mind as a result of looking at the cloud. If so, God is an attribute of Wordsworth's brain or exists somewhere in the relation between Wordsworth's brain and the cloud. And even if a higher reality, beyond the usual grasp of the human brain, is in truth communicating to Wordsworth from the cloud, this might still have been some biological harmony having no spiritual significance at all.

But suppose we say that this is all cavilling; suppose we say that Wordsworth's emotion is so sublime and impressive that we accept his use of the word God in this passage, what does it mean? Why the living God? What could God be if not merely 'alive', but eternal? The epithet suggests that Wordsworth must be referring to some deity other than the one personal God of the Christian Gospels, a kind of deity who could be either dead or alive. If so, what God? We are not told. And if Wordsworth is really referring to the personal God of Christianity, whom Herbert worshipped, we arrived at his meaning in spite of rather than because of his words. And if this is his meaning, how does the contemplation of a cloud transcend the offices of prayer? Can Wordsworth, then, only communicate with God under certain meteorological conditions?

This passage is taken from a recent number of *The Criterion* (Oct. 1932). I may remark to begin with that it is uncomfortably *not* surprising that this new Defender of the Faith, writing on Nicholas Ferrar and George Herbert, in a periodical known for its Anglo-Catholic tendency, should show himself ignorant of the language of the Book of Common Prayer. 'Why the living God?' Because Wordsworth knew his Psalms:

Like as the hart desireth the water-brooks,
So longeth my soul after thee, O God.
My soul is athirst for God, yea even for the living God;
When shall I come to appear before the presence of God?

> (Psalm 42, *Quemadmodum*,
> The Evening of the 8th Day.)

In the First Prayer Book of Edward VI this psalm was part of the order for the burial of the dead.[1]   And is Matthew xvi. 16 too recondite a reference?

We may note now, first, that Wordsworth's poem does not claim to transcend prayer and praise.   An experience is described in it as doing so—that is all. As to whether Wordsworth 'really felt these very emotions' and when: is the distinction between a poem and an autobiographical note, or an *affidavit*, really so difficult as this?   And, as to the next set of difficulties: what is there about Wordsworth's lines which specially invites them?   These are 'elementary questions' indeed, so elementary that any human utterance of any kind brings them up. Nothing in Herbert or Donne, or any other poet, is a whit more immune from them.   They must be reflected on by anyone who would read any poetry with sincerity.   But to use them as missiles in this fashion is merely to show lack of acquaintance with them *as questions*, as 'preliminary steps of the Methodical scale, at the top of which sits the author, and at the bottom the critic' (*Treatise on Method*, Snyder, 32).

However, this writer has been making some attempts to find out about these things.   He continues on a later page:

> Emotion in itself has no religious significance: an emotion is merely a reaction of feeling in the mental

---

[1] It remains, in Latin, in the Roman Catholic Office for the Dead. The phrase may also be found in the Canon of the Mass.

plane, as spontaneous as feelings of the physical senses.
The *Encyclopædia of Religion and Ethics,* in summing up
the view of emotion so far given by moral philosophy,
says that emotion cannot in itself be moral or immoral,
religious or irreligious: it only is the manner in which
the intellect judges and the will controls the emotions,
that can have a place among religious values. In
another place in the *Prelude,* Wordsworth does attempt
to give some such comment on the emotions, with the
following result. He is describing a child listening to a
singing shell:

> . . . and his countenance soon
> Brightened with joy; for from within were heard
> Murmurings, whereby the monitor expressed
> Mysterious union with its native sea.
> Even such a shell the universe itself
> Is to the ear of Faith: and there are times,
> I doubt not, when to you it doth import
> Authentic tidings of invisible things;
> Of ebb and flow, and ever during power;
> And central peace, subsisting at the heart
> Of endless agitation.

But what is it in fact that a child hears, or you
hear, when a shell is put to the ear? Not murmurings by which the monitor expresses mysterious
union with the sea, but in actual fact murmurings
which are the blood circulation in the listener's *own*
head. To apply Wordsworth's illustration, as he
asks us to apply it, what then are these 'authentic
tidings' that he draws from nature? Something, for
which a buzzing in his own head is his own chosen
simile.

Had Wordsworth paused to reflect and to judge,
instead of being swept away by emotions, he could never
have misapplied this elementary fact at this crucial

moment. Had he reflected and judged, he would have
rather written with Hopkins:

> Elected silence sing to me
> And beat upon my whirled ear.

And once the mind appreciates the collapse of
meaning, it can only turn from this passage and from
all the other passages that it represents, with something
of sense of failure and frustration, and even a loss of
pleasure in the poetry itself.

The 'collapse of meaning' however, is not in
Wordsworth but in this critic's reading of him. The
passage cited is, of course, on Coleridge's Wind
Harp theme again, an allegorical presentation of
the central problem of philosophy. The reader has
missed Wordsworth's deep self-critical humour, and
so laughs *at* the lines when he should smile with
them. To suggest that Wordsworth did not 'pause
to reflect and judge' shows an odd ignorance of
this poet's habits in composition.

It is amusing to observe that he gives, 'by way of
comparison', as an example of 'exact and careful
reflection', this image, which refers to Herbert's own
power of thought:

> Mark how the fire in flints doth quiet lie,
> Content and warm to itself alone.
> But when it would appear to other's eye
> Without a knock it never shone.

If Wordsworth had written this, how easily would
the reader have pointed out that the fire is not in
the flint but in the detached particle!

I have lingered with this example partly because it shows the kind of comment which Coleridge's doctrine, in my interpretation of it, must expect, but chiefly because it illustrates both erratic reading and lack of reflection upon the problems of symbolisation. There is a connection between these to-day which perhaps did not hold in former times. The capacity to read intelligently seems undoubtedly to have been greater among educated men in Coleridge's time than it is to-day. Three reasons at least may be suggested for this. More rigorous translation exercises in the schools; less shoddy reading material in our daily intake of printed matter; a greater homogeneity in the intellectual tradition. Only this last concerns us here. Intellectual tradition tells us, among other things, *how literally* to read a passage. It guides us in our metaphorical, allegorical, symbolical modes of interpretation. The hierarchy of these modes is elaborate and variable; and to read aright we need to shift with an at present indescribable adroitness and celerity from one mode to another. Our sixteenth- and seventeenth-century literature, supported by practice in listening to sermons and by conventions in speech and letter-writing which made 'direct' statement rare to a point which seems to us unnatural, gave an extraordinary training [1] in this skill. But it was skill merely; it was

[1] As Coleridge was among the first to point out, " Shakespeare's time, when the English Court was still foster-mother of the State and the Muses; and when, in consequence, the courtiers and men of rank and fashion affected a display of wit, point, and sententious

not followed up by theory. With the eighteenth century, the variety of the modes of metaphor in speech and in writing rapidly declined. Dr Johnson, for example, can show, at times, strange obtuseness in distinguishing between degrees of metaphor. It was this which made Donne seem artificial, absurd, unimpassioned and bewildering to him. But at the same time it is Johnson perhaps who shows us best the first steps of that reflective analytical scrutiny and comparison of the structures of meanings in poetry which is later to take a vast stride in Coleridge. For example, on these lines of Denham,

> O could I flow like thee, and make thy stream
> My great example as it is my theme!
> Though deep, yet clear; though gentle, yet not dull;
> Strong without rage, without o'erflowing full.

he remarks, "The lines are in themselves not perfect; for most of the words thus artfully opposed, are to be understood simply on one side of the comparison, and metaphorically on the other; and, if there be any language which does not express intellectual operations by material images, into that language they cannot be translated." There is, of course, no such language; but that Johnson should be applying such reflections to the analysis of

observation, that would be deemed intolerable at present—but in which a hundred years of controversy, involving every great political, and every dear domestic interest, had trained all but the lowest classes to participate. Add to this the very style of the sermons of the time, and the eagerness of the Protestants to distinguish themselves by long and frequent preaching, and it will be found that, from the reign of Henry VIII to the abdication of James II, no country ever received such a national education as England" (Raysor, I, 93.)

poetry is instructive. A more persistent examination would have shown him that the transferences here were sometimes primary, sometimes secondary, sometimes went from the river to the mind, sometimes from the mind to the river. And, with that, the assumptions behind his first remark would have been broken down. Naturally enough an age which, partly through false theory, partly through social causes, is losing its skill in interpretation, begins the reflective inquiry which may lead to a theory by which the skill may be regained—this time as a less vulnerable and more deeply grounded, because more consciously recognized, endowment.

With Coleridge's generation came a recovery of skill, both in readers and writers. It was maintained —for modes of meaning close in structure to those in Wordsworth, Shelley or Keats—until towards the end of the nineteenth century. Then came a sudden decline in performance. Twentieth-century criticism has been marked not so much by any enlightening reaction against the biassed preferences of the nineteenth century, as by the betrayal of general inability to read anything with safety on the part of most of those who have anything to say. Scholars and textual critics escape this generalization; but then professional students rarely have much to say. 'The true atheist is he whose hands are cauterized with holy things.' Their work is probably better in quality than any in the past—but we must recall that, like men of science, they have a cumulative advantage in technique, and they are also in closer contact with the records of tradition. Unluckily they have usually so much the less touch with its new shoots. And they rarely have voices that can be heard—a fact which may be a gain to the world. For if one asks, 'What can a lifetime of literary studies do towards judgment of the new?' the answer must, I fear, be a grim one. Thus the criticism that shapes public taste, and that may indirectly here and there influence original writing, is written by men of letters who are not primarily scholars. And it is this criticism that shows, I think demonstrably—though I decline the invidious task of demonstration—an alarming general drop in the capacity to construe the poetry which it discusses. Our 'Neo-Classic' age is repeating those feats of its predecessor which we least applaud. It is showing a fascinating versatility in travesty. And the poets of the 'Romantic' period provide for it what Shakespeare, Milton and Donne were to the early eighteenth-century grammarians and emendators—effigies to be shot at because what they represent is no longer understood. So the Chinese student bicycles to-day gaily and ribaldly round on the Altar of Heaven.

My point, however, is more general than these graceless and querulous remarks would suggest. It is that a great diversity in our current intellectual tradition, sharp opposition between its different branches, discontinuity in the process by which readers find themselves living in and with one or other of them, quick changes between them, insufficiently realized as they occur—in short, a general heterogeneity in our recent growth has disordered the conduct of reading. This shows itself most clearly, I think, in the frequency with which new and old-fashioned critics alike now pretend that their own inability to understand a poem is a sound argument against it. The conservatives use this plea against the new-fanglers quite as naïvely as do these against Shelley, Keats or Wordsworth. Both, of course, claim to be thereby upholding tradition. And both, to an onlooker, add sanction to Coleridge's adage, "Until you understand a writer's ignorance, presume yourself ignorant of his understanding."

The explanation of this embarrassing situation is not, I believe, in any fundamental difference in outlook between, say, Mr T. S. Eliot and Mr F. L. Lucas. No such gap separates them as divided Shelley from Dr Johnson. Yet something impenetrably shrouds Mr Eliot's constant preoccupation with the sources of nobility from Mr Lucas' eye; and something has at times hidden from Mr Eliot even those purposes of some romantic poetry which most resembled his own. I am tempted to connect these obstructions, to trace them to a common origin in divergent attitudes to language, to different ways in which words are used, and in which they are assumed to work.

Contemporary poetry (and very much of the poetry of other times in which contemporary readers are most interested) is generally supposed to be difficult. It will be fitting to conclude this examination of Coleridge's critical theories by considering what light they can throw upon this 'difficulty'. For it seems probable that in a large measure it derives from differences between the *actual* structures of the meanings of the poetry and the structures which, in various ways, are *supposed* to be natural and necessary to poetry, the structures which from habit and implicit theory are expected in its meanings.

But we must not confuse changes in the structures of poetic meanings with changes in the theories historically connected with them. Most theorizing upon meanings only very distantly reflects them. And this is our difficulty—with which Coleridge may help us. The technique of comparing the structures of meanings is still embryonic and much impeded by immature theories, due to the poets and others, as to what different kinds of poetry try to do and how they try to do it. In almost all familiar formulations, unreal problems of the *what* and of the *how* are distressingly entangled.

It is with deceptive ease, indeed, that the inquiry divides into questions about the *what* and the *how*. Or into questions about the *methods* a poet uses and the *feats* he thereby achieves. Or into questions about his *means* and his *ends*. Or about the *way* of his work and the *whither*. This ease is deceptive because, although for some purposes the division is necessary and for others convenient, in an examination of poetic structure the distinction prevents all advance by destroying the specimens we would examine.

How it does so may be best shown, perhaps, by taking the last of these formulations—between the *way* and the *whither* of a poem—and making the metaphor in it as explicit as possible, undeterred by any charges of 'intoxication by the obvious' that may be occasioned.

The metaphor is that of a path leading to some destination, or of a missile (arrow or boomerang) going to some mark; but let us exercise a trifling ingenuity in inventing journeys without destinations —movements of the earth, the pigeons' flight, the tacking of a boat, an ant's tour of the spokes of a wheel—or in considering the different trajectories which an arrow will take in shifting winds, or that most illuminating instance here, the rocket; and we shall see clearly how unnecessary, as applying to poems, the assumptions behind any division between a *way* and a *whither* may be. However widely we generalize it (as means and ends) the division is here an impeding product of abstraction. From the *total meaning* of the poem, we have singled out some component to be treated as its *whither* and to be set over against the rest as its *way*. We have chosen something to be, in a narrower sense, its 'meaning' and left the rest to be either the vehicle of this meaning or our further response to it. And until and unless we are explicitly aware of these processess of singling-out partial meanings we can make no progress in comparative studies of poetic structures.

Traditionally or conventionally the *whither* of a poem has often been taken to be 'what it says': and this, when thus singled out, has as often, in recent times, been regarded as of minor importance. As Professor Housman put it in his Leslie Stephen Lecture (*The Name and Nature of Poetry*, p. 37), "Poetry is not the thing said but a way of saying it." But this 'thing said', if we try with most poetry to separate it from the 'way of saying it', shows itself to be a most arbitrary thing. Unless we are unreasonably stern with it (or hold indefensible views on synonymity) we have to admit that even very slight changes in a way of saying anything *in poetry* change the thing said—and usually in evident and analysable respects. Only in abstracter matters than poetry ever touches is 'the same thought' able to be uttered with different words. But by taking 'the same thought' in a loose indefinite sense—as thoughts linked by a mere resemblance of topic—we can sometimes deceive ourselves and make the division between 'the thing said' and the 'way of saying it' seem useful and applicable.

"'But no man may deliver his brother, nor make agreement unto God for him', that," said Mr Housman, "is to me poetry so moving that I can hardly keep my voice steady in reading it. And that this is the effect of language I can ascertain by experiment: the same thought in the Bible version, 'None of them can by any means redeem his brother, nor give to God a ransom for him', I can read without emotion" (p. 37). That this is the effect of language we may grant without misgiving, but in what sense of *thought* that could be relevant do they utter the same thought? *Deliver—redeem; make agreement unto—give a ransom for:* the dominant metaphors are changed, and a defined explicit transaction has taken the place of a crowd of various or conflicting possibilities. It is surprising that so severe a textual critic and so rigorous an upholder of precision in literary studies as Mr Housman should permit himself such an opinion. The ambiguity of *thought* and its power to mislead even the most wary could not be better shown.

This 'thing said' is an abstraction from the whole meaning, and we may abstract it in various ways, taking a smaller or larger part of the whole meaning to be thus set over against the rest, and to be labelled, if we like, the poem's 'thought' or 'prose-sense'. Mr Housman calls it sometimes the 'intellectual content' sometimes simply the 'meaning'. Whatever the name, it is clear both that different readers will, with the same poem, separate different parts of the total meaning as this prose-sense; and that different poems invite different kinds of division in this respect. Sometimes the prose-sense seems to be the source, sometimes a tributary, sometimes a mere bank or dyke for the rest. These variations, from poem to poem, in the place and functions of the prose-sense, thought or 'meaning'—are by far the most accessible and examinable aspects of poetic structure. Yet to these differences the difficulty of 'understanding' poetry seems chiefly due. To understand a poem, in this sense, would be to permit the varied components of its total meaning to take their rightful places within it.

The besetting vice of all criticism is thus described by Coleridge—perhaps more clearly than by any other writer:

> We call, for we see and feel, the swan and the dove both transcendently beautiful. As absurd as it would be to institute a comparison between their separate claims to beauty from any abstract rule common to both, without reference to the life and being of the animals themselves—say rather if, having first seen the dove, we abstracted its outlines, gave them a false generalization, called them principle or ideal of bird-beauty and then proceeded to criticize the swan or the eagle—not less absurd is it to pass judgement on the works of a poet on the mere ground that they have been called by the same class-name with the works of other poets of other times and circumstances, or any ground indeed save that of their inappropriateness to their own end and being, their want of significance, as symbol and physiognomy (Raysor, I, 196).

The next step is to explore further the physiology, as it were, of poetry. In what we are apt to regard as the normal standard case, the prose-sense appears to be the source of the rest of our response.

> The Curfew tolls the knell of parting day,
>   The lowing herd wind slowly o'er the lea,
> The plowman homeward plods his weary way,
>   And leaves the world to darkness and to me.

Here everything which we need to think of is named by the words and described by the syntax, and any inferences we may add—that the poet is not weary as the ploughman is, or that the death of the day is to be compared with the end of their day of life for those lying in the churchyard—are fully prepared by this prose-sense. And, though it is, of course, merely by a figure of speech that we say that any one kind of component in a total meaning comes *before* another, it is clear that almost all the rest can be properly regarded as dependent from and controlled by the prose-sense here.

Now let us take a different case, Blake's song:

> Memory, hither come,
>   And tune your merry notes:
> And, while upon the wind
>   Your music floats,
> I'll pore upon the stream,
> Where sighing lovers dream,
> And fish for fancies as they pass
> Within the watery glass.

It is not hard to see that this has in some way a different structure. What is hard—but still must be attempted—is to say without exaggeration how its structure differs.

Some differences may be shown by these observations: that, if we abstract a plain sense from it, what we get is something very unlike, if separately considered, anything we are distinctly aware of in reading the words as poetry; secondly, that what prose-sense we obtain will be to some degree optional, will depend upon how we choose to interpret certain of the words in it. For example, *tune* may be read as 'sing, utter' or as 'accord, bring into order', *the stream* may be the 'mere river' or 'the stream of life, or time, or desire,' and *glass* may show merely the translucency of the water or turn it into an image-making reflection of things, as with a crystal we gaze into. But still, whatever we get from the poem as its *Sense*—whether, at one extreme, we make it merely an announcement of an intended revery, or, at the other, we load it with symbolic interpretations and make it a commentary on the theme, 'The Temporal the All'— what we get still stands over against the actual whole poetic meaning which any good reader knows as he reads it. The sense, however elaborated, remains something which does not *explain* the poetic meaning as the sense in the lines from the *Elegy* does explain their poetic meaning.

There is another fashion, of course, in which the sense may 'explain' the meaning. If we were asked, for example, 'How did Napoleon do all he did?' and replied, 'Because he was a great man!' our answer would not be an explanation in the stricter sense. But it might be an 'explanation' in the sense of being another way of saying how what he did strikes us as remarkable. Most explanations of poems are perhaps to be regarded as parallel to this, they are comments upon, not accounts of, the total meaning.

Observing this inadequacy or seeming irrelevance

of the prose-sense, we shall perhaps be tempted to say that the poem has no sense, no meaning, no intellectual content. The strength of the temptation is shown by the fact that so strict a reader as Mr Housman—for I have taken this example from him—did very nearly say this. He said (p. 43):

> That answers to nothing real; memory's merry notes and the rest are empty phrases, not things to be imagined; the stanza does but entangle the reader in a net of thoughtless delight.

But are there really any 'empty phrases' in it; and is the delight so 'thoughtless' after all? For, granting that no prose-sense we can extract from it is an adequate reflection of it, it is undeniable that all the main words in it have sense. And that their senses are directly relevant to the total meaning is shown by this: that if we change in the least their susceptibility to take certain senses the whole poem collapses. Though experience shows that such experiments are highly resented by some (but any temporary damage to the poem is slight and evanescent in healthy minds) let us try replacing *stream* by *steam*. Or let us read *watery glass* in a sense consonant rather with beer than with a rivulet. Who will doubt, after such trials, that these words *in the poem* have very definite senses in delicate interaction with those of the other words? But this is not to say that the whole poem derives simply from the articulation of these senses (as was almost the case with Gray); that would be to go too far in the opposite direction. The senses of the words here come to them as much from their feelings (to use this term as a convenient abbreviation for 'the rest of their powers upon us') as their feelings come from their senses. The interchange here seems nearly equal. But even in a case where feeling wholly dominates sense, it would not be true to say that the words, if they did receive some sense from feeling, were empty phrases. And cases where no sense, by whatever means, is given to the words, are extremely rare if indeed they occur at all. Of course, to use a sense in our reading is not the same thing as to be aware in reflection that we are doing so.

Not until we have set aside these two opposite misconceptions: that the whole meaning of a poem is or should be always simply derivative from its articulated prose-sense (if it has one): and that it can consist (for any length) of 'empty phrases'; can we examine poetic structures with any hope of discovering what may be happening.

Of the two errors the second is, at present, by far the most probable. It derives from that ambiguity of the word 'meaning' which leads us to suppose that if a poem has no articulated prose-sense (or none of independent importance) it has no meaning—confusing this narrower use with a wider use of 'meaning'. In the wider sense there are no meaningless poems, as, in the narrower sense, there are few meaningless words, even in the least articulated poems.

Blake's song, more perhaps even than most songs, is *dramatic*. That is, someone other than the poet is speaking (or the poet as other than the man). To take a long shot in a field to which guesses only are admitted, the melancholy Jacques is speaking. For is not this song a descendant of *As You Like It*, as *The Mad Song* is of the Storm Scene of *King Lear*, or Mr de la Mare's *Mad Prince's Song* is of *Hamlet*? However this may be, some poems are obviously more dramatic than others. By some we are invited to identify their voices with their authors'; others lend a character to or take one from other spokesmen; yet others, transcending personality, seem utterable only by

> Miracle, bird or golden handiwork.

Behind these large and apparent differences hosts of contributory and derivative microscopic changes of structure may well be suspected. For example, so abstruse a poem as Mr Yeats' magnificent *Byzantium* [1] might, if we were to take Mr Yeats to be speaking—and if the poem had not passed 'into the artifice of eternity'—challenge us to request explanations. But since the Superhuman, the Death-in-Life and Life-in-Death, is speaking, if we cannot 'understand' it, there will be no help for us from less authorities. The impersonality should there protect us from the impertinences and pedantries of our lesser selves.

[1] I agree with Mr Eliot, *The Use of Poetry*, p. 140, that in *Science and Poetry* I did not properly appreciate Mr Yeats' later work. I can plead that I wrote before *The Tower* was published.

All poetry (as all utterances) *can* of course be looked on as dramatic; but some poems more invite such reading than others and when so read are best understood. For example, Hopkins is most often non-dramatic, he speaks for himself. Mr Eliot's poems, on the other hand, are almost always dramatic. It is evident that if we simply and uniformly identify with the poet all poetry not plainly labelled 'Dramatic' we shall perpetrate much misreading—especially with modern poets. This is so patent that I am almost ashamed to write it, and I sympathize with my reader if it irks him; but such points cannot be taken for granted when critics of repute complain, for example, that Mr Eliot is far too young a man to compare himself with an 'aged eagle' (*Ash Wednesday*), or that he actually wishes to be a live lobster,[1] or that, since he is self-confessed a Hollow Man, 'headpiece stuffed with straw', no one should pay attention to him. And if these points of structure are so misconceived it will not be surprising if over-simple views prevail on finer points.

Many such critical preconceptions can be traced to mistaken endeavours to exalt poetry. 'It should come from the heart,' *i.e.* the poet is unpacking his heart in words. Or 'The more mysterious its action, the finer it probably is', *i.e.* explanation is belittling.

---

[1] *Prufrock*:

> I should have been a pair of ragged claws
> Scuttling across the floors of silent seas

—it should be a crab, I think, for crabs go sideways, which is the point.

This last seems often to favour the neglect of the prose-sense of poetry even when it is perfectly plain and evidently active in the meaning. A curious, but not uncommon, case is when the evident sense is accepted in the poetic reading but denied in the account afterwards given of it. I choose my example from Mr Housman (*The Name and Nature of Poetry*, p. 46).

In these six simple words of Milton:

Nymphs and shepherds, dance no more—

What is it that can draw tears, as I know it can, to the eyes of more readers than one? What in the world is there to cry about? Why have the mere words the physical effect of pathos when the sense of the passage is blithe and gay? I can only say, because they are poetry, and find their way to something in man which is obscure and latent, something older than the present organization of his nature, like the patches of fen which still linger here and there in the drained lands of Cambridgeshire.

Surely there is much more to say than this? Are these words really inexplicable in their effect or even at all hard to explain? And is 'the sense of the passage' really 'blithe and gay'? To say so, seems to me to overlook all the force of the words 'no more'. Lear's 'Thou'lt come no more' is the supreme instance. As Shenstone remarked (in 1761): "the words 'no more' have a singular pathos reminding us at once of past pleasure and the future exclusion of it." And the Nymphs and Shepherds that Milton pretends are going now to dance in England; we know, as he knew, that it is a pretence, that they have vanished; all that is over; and the dances in his *Masque* are no substitutes. Is the line lessened if we notice this? Is it not better to recognize that words work in intelligible (if intricate) ways than to appeal to a modern taste for primitiveness? And yet this very appeal has here taken a form which inversely reflects the very sense Milton put into his line.

While I am at this point, let me demur to one other implication in Mr Housman's treatment. Of Blake's

Hear the voice of the Bard!

he says, "that mysterious grandeur would be less grand if it were less mysterious; if the embryo ideas which are all that it contains should endue form and outline, and suggestion condense itself into thought."

'Embryo ideas' would be undeveloped ideas. There is a slighting implication in this description of them, whether or no we recall Milton's list of the destined contents of Limbo:

Embryos, and Idiots, Eremits and Friers
White, Black and Grey, with all their trumperie.

An embryo is at least a piteous and helpless thing, and commonly a parasite. And it is not certain at all here that the thought is dependent. Is it not equally likely that the ideas from which this poem derives its mysterious grandeur are not less but more fully developed as we receive them in the poem? I would suggest seriously that in the greater poems of great poets the ideas there brought into being in the mind are completer, not less complete; and that the process which extricates them by abstraction denatures them rather than develops them. The extracted abstract doctrine (if we arrive at any such) is a skeleton of the living knowledge, deformed and schematized for the legitimate purposes of comparison (as well as for the irrelevant purposes of argument). In the poem they are autonomous, sanctioned by their acceptability to the whole being of the reader. Out of the poem, they are doctrine merely, and a temptation to dispute.

But this perhaps is not so different as it seems from something Mr Housman may have been implying. I have wished only to protest, on Blake's behalf, against an arrogant 'intellectualist' assumption that the word 'embryo' *may* introduce. Blake knew what he was doing when he wrote about these things in verse, not prose. But we do not know what he was doing if we think he was not speaking —for and to the whole man, not the abstractive analytic intellect only—about the most important things in the world,

Of what is past, or passing, or to come.

To return to the division of the *way* and the *whither*; however we divide them, whether we make thoughts the way to the rest of the poem, or the rest of it the way to the thought—we shall, if we put the value of the poem either in the way or the whither, for most poems misconceive it. We may *read* them aright but we shall describe them wrongly. No great matter in itself perhaps; but, as we may see, these errors are small-scale models for enormous evils. As we habitually mistake our lesser myths, so we warp our world-picture by attempting amiss to 'understand' it, or by denying it all intelligibility, all meaning, because it lacks a certain sub-variety of meaning in the place in which we crave it. And, as with poetry, so with every mode of the mythopœic activity by which we live, shape universes to live in, reshape, inquire, in a thousand varying ways, seek

> patiently to bend
> Our mind to sifting reason, and clear light
> That strangely figured in our soul doth wend,
> Shifting its forms, still playing in our sight
> Till something it present that we shall take for right.[1]

We wrong it and thus ourselves if we take, as its 'point', some singled-out component only and disregard the rest. Yet having done this, by tradition, so long, we must now by conscious reflection compare the structures of different kinds of experience as of different kinds of poetry. Tradition, never really very successful in this, can no longer teach us even what it could—now that we live in a confluence of so many and such different streams. Our remedy, if we are not increasingly to misunderstand one another (thus misunderstanding ourselves), is the dangerous one of analysis; but it is dangerous only when we take the divisions we make as established

[1] Henry More, *Song of the Soul.*

insurmountably in the order of things, and not as introduced to assist us to compare.

What I have been urging as to the opposition of the 'thing said' and the 'way of saying it' holds good, I think, of every other division we may make in comparing the structure of poems. They are useful if we do not then segregate the value of the poem into some compartment thus created. To do so is like saying that the point of an elephant is his strength. (See Coleridge's remarks about the dove and the swan, cited above.) Apart from some forms of applied poetry—some satires or some devotional poems for example—poetry has no whither as opposed to a way. As Coleridge said in his description of a 'just poem' (*B. L.*, II, 11):

> The reader should be carried forward, not merely or chiefly by the mechanical impulse of curiosity, or a restless desire to arrive at the final solution; but by the pleasurable activity of mind excited by the attractions of the journey itself.

With the best poetry there is nowhere to arrive, no final solution. The poem is no ticket to the Fortunate Isles, or even to Purgatory, or even to Moscow. The journey is its own end, and it will not, by having no destination, any less assist the world to become what Moscow should be.

Poems which have a destination, a final solution—whether it be the enunciation of a supposed truth, or suasion to a policy, or the attainment of an end-state of consciousness, or some temporary or permanent exclusive attitude to the world, to society, or to the self, have only a subordinate value. Instead of establishing, as the best poetry does, the norms of value, they have to be judged by standards more inclusive than themselves—a consideration very relevant to the supposed 'difficulty' of much good poetry where this difficulty is conceived as an objection to it. As Coleridge put it:

> The elder languages were fitter for poetry because they expressed only prominent ideas with clearness, the others but darkly. . . . Poetry gives most pleasure when only generally and not perfectly understood. It was so by me with Gray's "Bard" and Collins' Odes. The "Bard" once intoxicated me, and now I read it without pleasure. From this cause it is that what I call metaphysical poetry gives me so much delight (*Anima Pœtæ*, p. 5).

'The elder languages' I take, perhaps arbitrarily, to be 'Elizabethan' English, for example; and 'prominent ideas' are not necessarily the most important.

It would be extremely interesting to know just what Coleridge included in 'What I call metaphysical poetry' here. It was not what Johnson and others have called by that name, Cowley being excluded but not Donne, and much of Wordsworth, almost undoubtedly, being added. 'Only generally and not perfectly understood' is a phrase full of dangers, of course. Shift the sense of 'understood' only a little and it is an excuse for every vague, undisciplined and erratic type of reading, for the merest misty indulgence in unformed 'sentimental' revery. But no one who knows his Coleridge will suppose that he meant this. What he is pointing to is the superiority of the characteristic Shakespearian structure of meaning over the characteristic later eighteenth-century structures, or of Blake's over Southey's. And we may equally take him as pointing to the superiority of the poetic structures used by Mr Yeats in his recent poetry, in his best poetry by Mr Eliot, by Mr Auden or Mr Empson at their best, or by Hopkins—very different though these structures are—their superiority to, let us say, the characteristic structures used by Rupert Brooke or the chief representatives of 'Georgian Poetry'. The point of contrast can be put shortly by saying that Rupert Brooke's verse, in compàrison with Mr Eliot's, has no *inside*. Its ideas and other components, however varied, are all expressed with prominence; lovely though the display may be, it is a display, the reader is visiting an Exhibition of Poetic Products.

An idea which is expressed 'but darkly' need be neither a dim nor a vague one—but it will be one which we have to look for. It is sometimes thought that this very process of 'looking into' a poem is destructive of the poetic virtue. But whether this is so of course depends upon how we 'look in'— upon what sort of a process this is. Certainly the detective intelligence, or the Cross-word Puzzler's technique, are not proper methods in reading poetry. Something resembling them was, perhaps, a suitable mode of preparation for reading some of Mr Eliot's earlier poems, *Burbank* or *A Cooking Egg* or some parts of *The Waste Land* for example. Those who went through it, however, found that what they thus discovered—though its discovery may have been necessary for them—was no essential part of the poetry when this came to life. That it can nearly all be forgotten without loss to the poetry, shows perhaps that it was scaffolding for the poet, as well as for the reader. But apart altogether from this play of extrinsic explicit conjecture, there is another way of 'looking into' abstruse poetry—a receptive submission, which will perhaps *be reflected* in conjectures but into which inferences among these conjectures do not enter. For example, the differences between the opening lines of the first and last sections of Mr Eliot's *Ash Wednesday*:

> Because I do not hope to turn again

and

> Although I do not hope to turn again

in their joint context and their coterminous subcontexts, will come into full being for very few readers without movements of exploration and resultant ponderings that I should not care to attempt to reflect in even the most distant prose translation. And yet these very movements—untrackable as they perhaps are, and uninducible as they almost certainly are by any other words—are the very life of the poem. In these searchings for meanings of a certain sort its being consists.

The poem is a quest, and its virtue is not in anything said by it, or in the way in which it is said,
or in a meaning which is found, or even in what
is passed by in the search. For in this poem—to
quote two lines from Coleridge's *Constancy to an Ideal
Object* which is a meditation on the same theme—
as in so much of the later poetry of Mr Yeats,

> like strangers sheltering from a storm
> Hope and Despair meet in the porch of Death.

And though from their encounter comes

> strength beyond hope or despair
> Climbing the third stair

there is no account, in other terms than those of
poetry, to be given of how it comes. Again the
resemblance to the symbolism of Mr Yeats' *The
Winding Stair* is of more than slight or accidental
interest. Is it not remarkable that not only Mr
Yeats, in his later poetry, and Mr Eliot in his
public penances for the sins of every generation,

> Now at this birth season of decease

but Mr Auden also,

> O watcher in the dark, you wake
> Our dream of waking,

Mr Empson, with his

> So Semele desired her Deity

and D. H. Lawrence, in all his last poetry,

> Turning to death as I turn to beauty

should be 'thus devoted, concentrated in purpose'?

When Mr Eliot discusses, in prose, the place of meanings in poetry and the bearing of false ex- pectations about them on this alleged 'difficulty' of modern poetry, what he says, though very helpful, needs to be read with a lively awareness of the ambiguities of the word *meaning* and a clear understanding of the narrowed sense in which he is using it. I will quote the whole passage in which he discusses these points:

The difficulty of poetry (and modern poetry is supposed to be difficult) may be due to one of several reasons. First, there may be personal causes which make it im- possible for a poet to express himself in any but an obscure way; while this may be regrettable, we should be glad, I think, that the man has been able to express himself at all. Or difficulty may be due just to novelty: we know the ridicule accorded in turn to Wordsworth, Shelley and Keats, Tennyson and Browning—but must remark that Browning was the first to be *called* difficult; hostile critics of the earlier poets found them difficult, but called them silly. Or difficulty may be caused by the reader's having been told, or having suggested to himself, that the poem is going to prove difficult. The ordinary reader, when warned against the obscurity of a poem, is apt to be thrown into a state of consternation very unfavourable to poetic receptivity. Instead of beginning, as he should, in a state of sensitivity, he obfuscates his senses by the desire to be clever and to look very hard for something, he doesn't know what— or else by the desire not to be taken in. There is such a thing as stage fright, but what such readers have is pit or gallery fright. The more seasoned reader, he who has reached, in these matters, a state of greater *purity*, does not bother about understanding; not, at

218

least, at first. I know that some of the poetry to which I am most devoted is poetry which I did not understand at first reading; some is poetry which I am not sure I understand yet: for instance, Shakespeare's. And finally, there is the difficulty caused by the author's having left out something which the reader is used to finding; so that the reader, bewildered, gropes about for what is absent, and puzzles his head for a kind of 'meaning' which is not there, and is not meant to be there.

The chief use of the 'meaning' of a poem, in the ordinary sense, may be (for here again I am speaking of some kinds of poetry and not all) to satisfy one habit of the reader, to keep his mind diverted and quiet, while the poem does its work upon him: much as the imaginary burglar is always provided with a bit of nice meat for the house-dog. This is a normal situation of which I approve. But the minds of all poets do not work that way; some of them, assuming that there are other minds like their own, become impatient of this 'meaning' which seems superfluous, and perceive possibilities of intensity through its elimination.

The 'state of consternation', it may be remarked, wears off quickly for most readers—for those readers at least who would be likely, if not handicapped by it, to 'understand' the poem in the end. And the *purer* reader, if he does not, in one sense, 'bother about understanding' is still, in another sense, occupied with nothing else. But the modes of understanding are as many and as varied as the structures of meanings.

If we turn now from the mere recognition that no prepossessions that we can form can *prescribe* a structure for the meanings in poetry—and yet every poem is a fabric of meaning—a recognition to which Coleridge's account of Imagination inevitably leads us; and from the speculative analysis of the possibilities of diverse poetic structures—a task for the criticism of the future—to speculations upon the causes of changes in the structures most employed by poets of successive generations and from these to an attempt to divine the general direction of these changes, we shall find further reasons for thinking that Coleridge's 'philosophic' approach to criticism is helpful.

That there has been a general drift in human interests in the West through the last four centuries—in the modes of our current mythology and in the functions of its parts—is hardly to be doubted. It shows itself in innumerable ways: in the growth of Science and History, in our changing attitudes to Authority in all its forms, to the Bible, to Tradition (as a body of truth to be received because of its source), to custom (to be accepted because established), to parental opinion. . . . It shows itself conspicuously in the philosophic movement from Descartes to Kant and on again to modern pragmatism and logical positivism; less conspicuously perhaps in the change from Locke's psychology to Freud's; less conspicuously still in the widespread increase in the aptitude of the average mind for self-dissolving introspection,the generally heightened awareness of the goings on of our own minds, merely *as goings on*, not as transitions from one well-known and linguistically recognized moral or intellectual condition to another. And together with this last (it is an aspect of the same change) it shows itself in the startling enhancement of our interest in the *sensory* detail and *nuance* of the visible scene as opposed to the practically useful information about things which these perceptions can give us.

In these last modifications of consciousness we may see more clearly and less debatably than with the others what has been happening. They witness to a change in the focus of what Coleridge called 'the primary imagination . . . the living Power and prime Agent of all human Perception' (*B. L.*, I, 202) and are clearly enough reflected in those activities of character-drawing and description which are so large a part of the work of the 'secondary imagination' of the Novelist. I have in view a very obvious contrast between the modes of depicting both character and the landscape practised by the best seventeenth- and eighteenth-century writers and the best modern novelists. George Moore somewhere in *Avowals*, wishing to say something derogatory of *Tom Jones*, described it, if memory serves me, as 'an empty book without a glimpse of the world without or a hint of the world within'. The remark is perfectly true. There is neither an outer nor an inner world in *Tom Jones* as these are to be found in the work of modern novelists. We can hunt through it in vain to find either a scene described primarily in terms of its appearance, or however short a stretch of the 'stream of consciousness' given with the sensuous detail that any of a dozen modern writers could give it for us. And what is true of Fielding is true, with very rare exceptions, of all the greater seventeenth- and eighteenth-century writers. Defoe, for example, though he has plenty of descriptions, is never interested in the appearances of things for the sake of the appearances themselves or the reverberations of their *sensory* qualities in the percipient's mind. He is interested in the things and their condition, the help or hindrance they can be to man. To turn from his accounts of Crusoe's seashore to Mr Joyce's description of Sandymount strand is to realize how great a change in man's interests (and perhaps in his perceptions themselves) has occurred. And to turn from Crusoe's moralizing self-examinations to those of Stephen Dedalus is to notice the same change. As Crusoe's eyes, looking outwards, see things where Stephen's see symbols of his own moods; so, when he looks into his own heart he finds a clear-cut world of hopes and fears, doubts and faiths—complex indeed but as well defined in their interrelations as chessmen. There is no uncertainty as to which movements belong to which side. But Stephen's inner world is as phantasmagoric as his outer, being composed of images which shift and flow and merge with an intricacy beyond the survey of any moral principles and too subtle to be described in the terms of any hitherto conceived psychology. The nomenclature of the faculties, of the virtues and the vices, of the passions, of the moods, the whole machinery through which self-examination with a view to increased order could be conducted by Defoe, has lapsed.

We may suspect, with Coleridge, that for some time it has been no such loss as it may appear; and that some dissolution of it must precede a reconstruction:

> The "King And No King" too, is extremely spirited in all its Characters; Arbaces holds up a Mirror to all Men of Virtuous Principles but violent Passions: hence he is, as it were, at once Magnanimity and Pride, Patience and Fury, Gentleness and Rigor, Chastity and Incest, and is one of the finest Mixtures of Virtues and Vices that any Poet has drawn, &c. (*Preface to Seward's Edition of Beaumont and Fletcher*, 1750).

"These," Coleridge comments, "are among the endless instances of the abject state to which psychology had sunk from the reign of Charles I to the middle of the present reign of George III; and even now it is but just awaking." As chief awakener, he can speak with authority. Since his time the dissolution has gone further. The old vocabulary, from being a framework indispensable, but not necessarily sufficient, for orientation, has become a mere supply of words which, because of their past history, can be used as tinctures in the composition of states of mind to which none of them apply.

We are apt to regard this change as a great new conquest of literature over the unexplored land of ordinary human consciousness, overlooking perhaps

the other possibility that ordinary human consciousness may not, until recently, have had a form which
could be thus represented. And we are ready to
acclaim the descriptions of the visible scene which
Katherine Mansfield, Stella Benson or Virginia Woolf
can give us as showing a subtlety in the observation
of its sensory aspects and their emotional significance
which is disappointingly absent in earlier writers.
On one interpretation of the change, they have
improved the descriptive technique of prose, have
caught something always present which writers in
the past could not (or did not wish to) catch; on
another interpretation something new in the modes
of perception has come into being for them to
describe. The two accounts are not perhaps so
opposed as they may seem, and I have no desire
to decide between them. On either account man's
interest in his own consciousness, whether of things
without him or of the movements of his own mind,
has changed, and with it the mode of an important
part of his mythology.

That this change should show itself most clearly
in prose is to be expected. For such prose as Mr
Joyce's or Mrs Woolf's is a dilution (or better, an
expansion, 'like gold to ayery thinnesse beate') of
a use of words that has in most ages been within
the range of poetry. What is new is the composition
of whole books with meanings of a structure which
in poetry is found only in phrases or single lines
supported by quite other structures. And these
other structures are strengthened by just those other

components which George Moore overlooked in reading *Tom Jones*. Empty though it is of 'glimpses of the world without or hints of the world within' it contains judgment, a moral order, and action, with all that these entail. It contains *ideas*, not as stimulants to revery and whimsy, but as assured forms of mental activity with which coherent purpose may be maintained. And though, as we have seen with the ideas (or doctrines) that may be extracted from Coleridge's Wind Harp image, we must not identify the abstracted idea with the idea *in* the poem, yet ideas in the completeness they have in poetry are commonly main components in its structure. *Tom Jones*, of course, is not a poem; but the components which enter into its prose-fabric and give it its power are of kinds which do not enter into *Jacob's Room* or *Ulysses*; and, otherwise disposed and interrelated, they are more essential parts of the structure of great poetry than those which do. For these are, as Coleridge would say, only 'the rudiments of imagination's power'.

The dissolution of consciousness exhibited in such prose, at its best as much as in merely imitative writing, forces the task of reconstituting a less relaxed, a less adventitious order for the mind upon contemporary poetry. There can be no question of a return to any mythologic structures prevailing before the seventeenth century. The depth of the changes that then took place (they are described with admirable detachment and clarity in Mr Basil

Willey's *The Seventeenth Century Background*) prevents return. Poetry can no more go back on its past than a man can.

But the waning of any one mode of order—a traditional morality, or a religious sanction or symbolization for it—is not the loss of all possibilities of order. The traditional schemas by which man gave an account of himself and the world in which he lived were made by him, and though they have lost their power to help him as they formerly helped him, he has not lost his power to make new ones. It is easy to represent what has been occurring as a course of error, as due to the pernicious influence of arrogant science, or of Cartesianism or of Rousseau; as an infection of the mind by 'heresies', or as departure from a norm to which, if man is to become again a noble animal, he must return. Dramas in which the proper balance of our faculties has been destroyed by exorbitant claims from one or other of them, in which science displaces religious belief, or sentiment ousts reason, or dreams cloud Reality,

> What will be forever
> What was from of old,

—by corruption from which disasters we now wander, a lost generation, in a wrecked universe—are not hard to invent.

> It was man did it, man
> Who imagined imagination;
> And he did what man can
> He uncreated creation

as Mr R. G. Eberhart exclaimed. But these dramatic pictures of our predicament are utterances of distress. Though they may sometimes pretend to be diagnoses, they are myths reflecting our unease. What they profess to describe is too vast a matter to be handled by that other system of myths (those of Science and History) to which diagnoses belong, and in which verification is possible. And as philosophic myths they are not of the kind which contribute directly to a new order. For the concepts they use belong to the order which has passed, and they are disqualified by the movement they describe. It is better, as an alternative philosophic myth, to suppose that the great drift is not due merely to internal conflicts between sub-orders of our mythology but rather to an inevitable growth of human awareness—inevitable because Man goes on and he retains, in recent centuries, increasing touch with his past.

To put the burden of constituting an order for our minds on the poet may seem unfair. It is not the philosopher, however, or the moralist who puts it on him, but birth. And it is only another aspect of the drift by which knowledge in all its varieties—scientific, moral, religious—has come to seem a vast mythology with its sub-orders divided according to their different pragmatic sanctions, that the poet should thus seem to increase so inordinately in importance. (There is a figure of speech here, of course, for the burden is not on individual poets but upon the poetic function. With Homer, Dante and Shakespeare in mind, however, the importance of the single poet is not to be under-estimated.) For while any part of the world-picture is regarded as not of mythopœic origin, poetry—earlier recognized as mythopœic—could not but be given a second place. If philosophic contemplation, or religious experience, or science gave us Reality, then poetry gave us something of less consequence, at best some sort of shadow. If we grant that all is myth, poetry, as the myth-making which most brings 'the whole soul of man into activity' (*B. L.*, II, 12), and as working with words, 'parts and germinations of the plant' and, through them, in 'the medium by which spirits communicate with one another' (*B. L.*, I, 168), becomes the necessary channel for the reconstitution of order.

But this last phrase is tainted also with a picturesque mock-desperate dramatization of our situation. The mind has never been in order. There is no vanished perfection of balance to be restored. The great ages of poetry have mostly been times torn by savage and stupid dissension, intolerant, unreasonable, and confused in other aspects of human endeavour.

> Allas, allas! now may men wepe and crye!
> For in our dayes nis but covetyse
> And doublenesse, and tresoun and envye,
> Poysoun, manslauhtre, and mordre in sondry wyse.

In all this our own age may be preparing to emulate them; but that is no more a reason to anticipate a new great age for poetry than the new possibility of a material paradise now offered by science is a reason for thinking that the day of poetry is over. Eras that produced no poetry that is remembered have been as disordered as ours. There are better reasons, in the work of modern poets, to hope that a creative movement is beginning and that poetry, freed from a mistaken conception of its limitations. and read more discerningly than heretofore, will remake our minds and with them our world. Such an estimate of the power of poetry may seem extravagant; but it was Milton's no less than Shelley's, Blake's or Wordsworth's. It has been the opinion of many with whom we need not be ashamed to agree: "The study of poetry (if we will trust Aristotle) offers to mankind a certain rule, and pattern, of living well and happily; disposing us to all civil offices of society. If we will believe Tully, it nourisheth and instructeth our youth; delights our age; adorns our prosperity; comforts our adversity; entertains us at home . . . insomuch as the wisest and best learned have thought her the absolute mistress of manners, and nearest of kin to virtue." Ben Jonson here may merely be repeating commonplaces from antiquity; he may be writing a set piece without concern for what he is saying—but this is unlikely; he may not have been aware of the reasons for such opinions; they were left for Coleridge to display; but he was certainly well placed to judge whether they were creditable opinions or not. Neither the authorities he cites, nor 'this robust, surly, and observing dramatist' himself, may be thought insufficiently acquainted with ordinary lives, or with the forces that may amend them.

Poetry may have these powers and yet, for removable and preventable causes, the study of poetry be of no great use to us. A candid witness must declare, I fear, that its benefits are often unobtrusive where we would most expect them. But the study of poetry, for those born in this age, is more arduous than we suppose. It is therefore rare. Many other things pass by its name and are encouraged to its detriment.

To free it from distracting trivialities, from literary chit-chat, from discussion of form which does not ask what has the form, from flattening rationalization, from the clouds of unchecked sensibility and unexamined interpretations is a minor duty of criticism. But there is a more positive task: to recall that poetry is the supreme use of language, man's chief co-ordinating instrument, in the service of the most integral purposes of life; and to explore, with thoroughness, the intricacies of the modes of language as working modes of the mind.

The sage may teach a doctrine without words; but, if so, it is a doctrine about another world than ours and for another life. Our world and our life have grown and taken what order they have for us through separated meanings which we can only hold together or keep apart through words. The sage may avoid words because our power of controlling certain kinds of meaning through them is too slight; but without the use of words in the past he would have had no doctrine to teach. The meanings sufficient for the dumb creatures are not enough for man.

Because all objects which we can name or otherwise single out—the simplest objects of the senses and the most recondite entities that speculation can conjecture, the most abstract constructions of the intellect and the most concrete aims of passion alike—are projections of man's interests; because the Universe as it is known to us is a fabric whose forms, as we can alone know them, have arisen in and through reflection; and because that reflection, whether made by the intellect in science or by 'the whole soul of man' in poetry, has developed through language—and, apart from language, can neither be continued nor maintained—the study of the modes of language becomes, as it attempts to be thorough, the most fundamental and extensive of all inquiries. It is no preliminary or preparation for other profounder studies, which though they use language more or less trustfully, may be supposed to be autonomous, uninfluenced by verbal processes. The very formation of the objects which these studies propose to examine takes place through the processes (of which imagination and fancy are modes) by which the words they use acquire their meanings.

Criticism is the science of these meanings and the

meanings which larger groups of words may carry. It is no mere account of what men have written or how they have written it, taken as questions to be judged by borrowed standards or to be asked without inquiry into the little that we can yet surmise about the growth of the mind and therewith the expansion of our outlook on the world.

Thus the more traditional subjects of criticism, Coleridge's differentiation of imagination from fancy, and his still abstruser ponderings on objectification and the living word, unite with the analysis of the ambiguities and confusions that are overt or latent in all cases of metaphor, transference or projection to form one study. It is embryonic still, through which its possibilities are the less restricted. It offers little intellectual rest or satisfaction; but should we look for satisfaction here where all the problems meet? What it does offer is an immense opportunity for improving our technique of understanding.

With Coleridge we step across the threshold of a general theoretical study of language capable of opening to us new powers over our minds comparable to those which systematic physical inquiries are giving us over our environment. The step across was of the same type as that which took Galileo into the modern world. It requires the shift from a preoccupation with the What and Why to the How of language. The problems of Poetry became for Coleridge, sometimes, interesting as problems with a structure of their own. They ceased to be mere voids waiting to be filled. The interest shifted from the answers to the questions; and, with that, a new era for criticism began. Beyond the old tasks of reaffirming ancient conclusions and defending them from foolish interpretations, an illimitable field of work has become accessible.

The change would have been delayed if Coleridge had not been a philosopher as well as a critic. And it has this consequence, that critics in the future must have a theoretical equipment of a kind which has not been felt to be necessary in the past. (So physicists may at times sigh for the days in which less mathematics was required by them.) But the critical equipment will not be *primarily* philosophical. It will be rather a command of the methods of comparing our meanings. As the theory of Poetry develops, what is needed will be disengaged from philosophy much as the methodology of physics has been disengaged.

I have tried here to further this development by presenting Coleridge's Theory of Imagination for more detailed consideration than it has hitherto received, and by adding suggestions towards extensions of his method of analysis. These must perhaps await fuller exposition before they become effective. But, with the history of opinions on Coleridge before us, it seemed but just that an account of his work should be attempted before new derivations from it again obscure our debt.

INDEX

INDEX